Bruges
and Ghent

DIRECTIONS

WRITTEN AND RESEARCHED BY

Phil Lee

ROUGH
GUIDES

NEW YORK • LONDON • DELHI
www.roughguides.com

Contents

Introduction to

Bruges and Ghent

In 1896 the novelist and playwright Arnold Bennett complained, "The difference between Bruges and other cities is that in the latter you look about for the picturesque, while in Bruges, assailed on every side by the picturesque, you look curiously for the unpicturesque, and don't find it easily."

◄ Kwak beer

Perhaps so, but for the modern palate, battered by postwar development, Bruges's blend of antique architectural styles, from tiny brick cottages to gracious Classical mansions, is a welcome relief – and retreat. It certainly brings out the romance in many of its visitors – stay here long enough and you can't help but be amazed by the number of couples wandering its canals hand-in-hand, cheek-to-cheek. Neither does it matter much that a fair slice of Bruges is not quite what it seems: many buildings are not the genuine article, but are carefully constructed to resemble their medieval predecessors. Bruges has spent time and money preserving its image, rendering almost everything that's new in various versions of medieval style, and the result is one of Europe's most beautiful city centres, whose charms are supplemented by a clutch of museums, plus lots of inviting restaurants and bars.

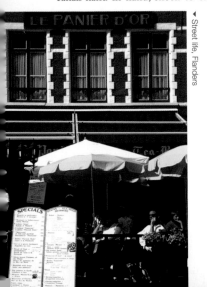

◄ Street life, Flanders

Neighbouring Ghent boasts its share of handsome medieval buildings too, and also possesses one of the artistic wonders of the medieval world, the *Adoration of the Mystic Lamb* altarpiece by Jan

When to visit

Bruges and Ghent are all-year destinations, with most attractions and nearly all their bars and restaurants open in winter and summer alike. Both cities enjoy a fairly standard temperate climate, with warm, if mild, summers and cold winters, without much snow. The warmest months are usually June, July and August (averaging 18°C); the coldest, December and January (averaging 2°C), when short daylight hours and weak sunlight can make the weather seem colder (and wetter) than it actually is. Rain is always a possibility, even in summer, which actually has more rainfall than either autumn or winter. Warm days in April and May, when the light has the clarity of springtime, are especially appealing. In Bruges, however, the advantage of sunnier weather and longer daylight hours in July and August is offset by the excessive number of tourists. If you're planning a short visit, it's worth noting that almost all of the cities' museums are closed on Mondays.

van Eyck. Nonetheless, the atmosphere here is markedly different from that in Bruges, and the tourist industry supplements but does not dominate the local economy. As a consequence, Ghent preserves the raw and authentic edges that Bruges has tried so hard to iron out , its busy, bustling centre reflecting the to-ings and fro-ings of generations of merchants, weavers, industrialists and workers, as well as accommodating a thriving restaurant and bar scene.

In medieval times, both Bruges and Ghent prospered as lynchpins of the cloth trade, turning high-quality English wool into clothing that was exported all over the world. It was an immensely profitable business and one that made Bruges, in particular, a focus of international trade. Through the city's harbours, Flemish cloth was exchanged for hogs from Denmark, spices from Venice, hides from

▼ Chocolates, Bruges

Ireland, wax from Russia, gold and silver from Poland and furs from Bulgaria. However, despite (or perhaps because of) this lucrative state of affairs, Bruges and Ghent were dogged by war. The weavers and merchants of both cities were dependent on the goodwill of the kings of England for their wool supply, but their feudal overlords, the counts of Flanders and their successors the dukes of Burgundy, were vassals of the rival king of France. Consequently, whenever France and England were at war – which was often – both cities found themselves in a precarious position.

The Habsburgs swallowed Flanders – including both Bruges and Ghent – into their empire towards the end of the fifteenth century and the sour relations that existed between the new rulers and the two cities led to their decline. Economically and politically marooned, Bruges was especially hard hit and simply withered away, its houses deserted, its canals empty and its money spirited away by the departing merchants. Some four centuries later, Georges Rodenbach's novel *Bruges-la-Morte* alerted well-heeled Europeans to the town's aged, quiet charms, and Bruges attracted its first wave of tourists. Many of them – especially the British – settled here and came to play a leading role in preserving the city's architectural heritage and today Bruges is one of the most popular weekend destinations in Europe. Ghent, meanwhile, fared rather better, struggling on as a minor port and trading depot until its fortunes were revived by the development of a cotton spinning industry in the early years of the nineteenth century. Within the space of forty years, Ghent was jam-packed with factories producing all manner of industrial goods and, although the city has moved on from its industrial base, it remains economically buoyant and is Belgium's third largest metropolis with a population of around 250,000.

▼ Graslei, Ghent

Bruges and Ghent
AT A GLANCE

THE MARKT, BRUGES

At the centre of Bruges, this handsome cobbled square was long the commercial heart of the city, and is still home to one of the city's most striking medieval landmarks, the Belfort, whose distinctive lantern tower pierces the city's skyline.

◄ The Belfort, Bruges

▲ The Burg, Bruges

THE BURG, BRUGES

The city's second central square, the Burg is flanked by an especially beautiful group of buildings, including the postcard-perfect Gothic Stadhuis and the Heilig Bloed Basiliek, which holds the city's holiest relic, a phial purportedly containing a few drops of blood washed from the body of Christ.

SOUTH OF THE MARKT, BRUGES

The streets south of the Markt are home to several of the city's key sights, from the medieval Onze Lieve Vrouwekerk and St Janshospitaal, through to the whitewashed cottages of the Begijnhof and the Minnewater, the so-called "Lake of Love".

THE GROENINGE MUSEUM, BRUGES

The superb Groeninge Museum boasts one of the world's finest collections of early Flemish paintings, including works by Jan van Eyck, Rogier van der Weyden, Hans Memling and Hieronymus Bosch.

▲ Ghent Train station

NORTH AND EAST OF THE MARKT, BRUGES

The areas north and east of the centre are home to an especially beguiling collection of handsome streetscapes, with graceful mansions and intimate brick houses draped along a lattice of slender canals, crisscrossed by dinky little stone bridges.

DAMME

A popular day-trip from Bruges, the pretty little village of Damme perches beside a canal 7km to the northeast of the city.

◄ Canal near Damme

CENTRAL GHENT

Ghent's ancient centre holds a glorious set of Gothic buildings, including the stirring St Baafskathedraal (also home to the remarkable *Adoration of the Mystic Lamb* by Jan van Eyck), St Niklaaskerk, the medieval guild houses of the Graslei, and a forbidding castle, Het Gravensteen.

◄ Graslei, Ghent

SOUTHERN GHENT

Ghent's two leading art museums – the Museum voor Schone Kunsten and S.M.A.K. – are located a couple of kilometres south of the centre, not far from the main train station.

Ideas

The big six sights

Neither Bruges nor Ghent is packed with major sights: their real pleasures lie in their charming mix of antique buildings set against a skein of canals, all best absorbed by easy wanderings. Nevertheless, there are a number of attractions you shouldn't leave without seeing, ranging from the landmark Belfort overlooking Bruges's Markt through to Jan van Eyck's masterful *Adoration of the Mystic Lamb*, housed in Ghent's impressive cathedral.

▲ The Belfort

One of Belgium's most distinctive landmarks, the soaring lantern tower of the Belfort pierces the skyline of central Bruges.

P.51 ▶ THE MARKT, BRUGES

▲ Groeninge Museum

The city's leading museum, internationally famous for its collection of early Flemish paintings.

P.83–89 ▶ THE GROENINGE MUSEUM, BRUGES

▼ Sint Janshospitaal

This former hospital is now a museum housing a wonderful sample of the paintings of Hans Memling.

P.70 ▸ SOUTH OF THE MARKT, BRUGES

▼ Adoration of the Mystic Lamb

Displayed in Ghent's St Baafskathedraal, Jan van Eyck's visionary painting celebrates the Lamb of God, the symbol of Christ's sacrifice.

P.111 ▸ CENTRAL GHENT

▲ Heilig Bloed Basiliek

The city's most important shrine, home to the revered phial of the Holy Blood, its contents reputedly washed from the body of the crucified Christ.

P.57 ▸ THE BURG, BRUGES

▲ Onze Lieve Vrouwekerk

Topped by one of the tallest spires in Belgium, the rambling Onze Lieve Vrouwekerk is the pick of the city's medieval churches.

P.68 ▸ SOUTH OF THE MARKT, BRUGES

Canalside Bruges

Bruges is famous for its canals, those narrow waterways that lattice the city centre and provide a beautiful contrast with its antique buildings. Ornamental today, they were once the city's economic lifeline with ships sailing into the city from the North Sea via the canal that ran from Damme. There are boat tours of the central canals, but the prettiest stretches are often only to be reached on foot.

▲ Jan van Eyckplein

Once a centre of merchant life, this quiet square overlooks the Spiegelrei canal.

P.91 ▶ NORTH AND EAST OF THE MARKT, BRUGES

▼ St Bonifaciusbrug

No question, this is the quaintest bridge in Bruges – even if it was built in 1910.

P.67 ▶ SOUTH OF THE MARKT, BRUGES

▼ Gouden Handrei

Home to an eye-catching medley of those distinctive canalside outhouses that stand at the end of many city gardens.

P.93 ▸ NORTH AND EAST OF THE MARKT, BRUGES

▲ Minnewater

The "Lake of Love" attracts canoodlers by the score.

P.76 ▸ SOUTH OF THE MARKT, BRUGES

▼ Augustijnenbrug

The city's oldest bridge, named after the Augustinian monks who once lived nearby.

P.94 ▸ NORTH AND EAST OF THE MARKT, BRUGES

▲ Rozenhoedkaai

This slender quai provides an exquisite view of the Belfort.

P.64 ▸ SOUTH OF THE MARKT, BRUGES

Medieval Flemish art

Throughout the medieval period, Flanders was one of the most artistically productive parts of Europe, with all the Flemish cloth towns – and especially Bruges and Ghent – trying to outdo one another with the quality of their religious art. Today, the works of these early Flemish painters, are highly prized, and there's an excellent selection on display in both cities, most memorably in Bruges at the Groeninge Museum and in St Janshospitaal.

▲ Jan Provoost

Provoost packed a real punch into his paintings, as here, showing a miser attempting to bargain with death.

P.87 ▸ THE GROENINGE
　　　　MUSEUM, BRUGES

▲ Hieronymus Bosch

Bosch's religious allegories are filled with macabre visions of tortured people and grotesque beasts.

P.86 ▸ THE GROENINGE
　　　　MUSEUM, BRUGES

▲ Gerard David

Typical of the work of David, this triptych is a restrained meditation on the baptism of Christ.

P.86 ▶ THE GROENINGE MUSEUM, BRUGES

▶ Rogier van der Weyden

Weyden's serene portraits of religious scenes and local bigwigs were much admired across western Europe.

P.84 ▶ THE GROENINGE MUSEUM, BRUGES

◀ Jan van Eyck

Arguably the greatest of the early Flemish masters, van Eyck was a key figure in the development of oil painting, modulating its tones to create paintings of extraordinary clarity and realism.

P.83 ▶ THE GROENINGE MUSEUM, BRUGES

Modern Belgian art

René Magritte, one of Surrealism's leading lights, was Belgian, and his work exemplifies the country's enduring penchant for the bizarre and macabre – themes which can be traced back to the grotesques of James Ensor, and even Hieronymus Bosch. Similarly appealing to Belgian sensibilities was Expressionism, whose exaggerated shapes and colours are evident in the eye-catching canvases of Constant Permeke. The finest collections of modern Belgian art can be found at Ghent's Museum voor Schone Kunsten (see p.135) and S.M.A.K. (see p.134), and the Groeninge Museum (see p.83–89) in Bruges.

▲ **Fernand Khnopff**

Khnopff was Belgium's leading Symbolist, his unsettling canvases playing with notions of lust and desire.

P.89 ▸ THE GROENINGE MUSEUM, BRUGES

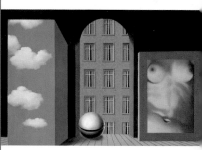

▲ **René Magritte**

Magritte used ordinary images in a dreamlike way, with strange, disconcerting juxtapositions.

P.136 ▸ SOUTHERN & EASTERN GHENT

▲ James Ensor

Ensor painted and drew grisly, disturbing
works – often of skulls and skeletons
– whose haunted style prefigured
Expressionism.

P.136 ▶ SOUTHERN & EASTERN
GHENT

▶ Constant Permeke

Belgium's leading Expressionist, whose bold,
deeply shaded canvases can be found in
many Belgian galleries.

P.89 ▶ THE GROENINGE MUSEUM,
BRUGES

Churches

Profoundly Catholic for most of their history, Bruges and Ghent possess a liberal sprinkling of churches. The finest are Gothic, built on the profits of the cloth trade and dating back to the thirteenth century, though these were all modified in later centuries – a tower here and an aisle there. The second major period of church building was in the nineteenth century, when the neo-Gothic style ruled the architectural roost.

▲ Jeruzalemkerk

The most unusual church in Bruges, surmounted by an idiosyncratic lantern tower.

P.96 ▶ NORTH AND EAST OF THE MARKT, BRUGES

▲ St Baafskathedraal

At the heart of Ghent, St Baafskathedraal is one of Belgium's finest Gothic churches.

P.109 ▶ CENTRAL GHENT

▼ St Walburgakerk

Handsome Baroque church built for the Jesuits in the seventeenth century.

P.94 ▶ NORTH AND EAST OF THE MARKT, BRUGES

▲ St Niklaaskerk

An exquisite example of early Gothic architecture, the angular lines of St Niklaaskerk rise high above Ghent.

P.114 ▶ CENTRAL GHENT

▶ St Salvatorskathedraal

A sterling Gothic edifice with a spectacular tower and an interior stuffed with all sorts of ecclesiastical bric-a-brac.

P.73 ▶ SOUTH OF THE MARKT, BRUGES

▼ Onze Lieve Vrouwekerk

This intriguing medieval church is home to a Michelango Madonna in the nave and two superbly crafted medieval sarcophagi in the choir.

P.68 ▶ SOUTH OF THE MARKT, BRUGES

19

Museums

Bruges's most important museums are the Groeninge (see p.83–89) and Sint Janshospitaal (see p.70), home to outstanding collections of fine art, but there are more old Flemish paintings in the intriguing Onze-Lieve-Vrouw ter Potterie museum. Bruges was once famous for its tapestries and there's a first-rate sample of them in the Gruuthuse, whilst lace – another Bruges speciality – is featured in the Kantcentum (Lace Centre). In Ghent, pride of place goes to the city's two main art galleries – S.M.A.K. (see p.134) and the Schone Kunsten (see p.135) – while the Design Museum has a striking collection of modern furnishings and fittings.

▼ Arentshuis

There are temporary exhibitions of fine and applied art here plus a permanent collection devoted to the painting and drawings of the Bruges-born artist Frank Brangwyn.

P.66 ▸ SOUTH OF THE MARKT, BRUGES

▼ Gruuthuse

The Gruuthuse holds an outstanding collection of applied art, including a raft of tapestries and a famous bust of Charles V.

P.68 ▸ SOUTH OF THE MARKT, BRUGES

▲ Kantcentrum

The Kantcentrum (Lace Centre) exhibits a
small collection of antique lace and hosts
informal demonstrations of traditional
lace-making

P.95 ▶ NORTH AND EAST OF THE
MARKT, BRUGES

▲ Design Museum

Period rooms at the front and contemporary
design at the back, make this one of Ghent's
most varied museums.

P.117 ▶ CENTRAL GHENT

▼ Onze-Lieve-Vrouw ter Potterie

This unusual museum, in a one-time
medieval hospital, includes a handsome
chapel with lovely stained-glass windows.

P.100 ▶ NORTH AND EAST OF THE
MARKT, BRUGES

Canalside hotels

Some of the classiest hotels in Bruges (plus a couple in Ghent) occupy charming canalside locations, offering delightful views from many of their guest and public rooms. The majority of these hotels occupy grand Neoclassical mansions, but some are in older brick buildings dating back to medieval times.

▲ Die Swaene, Bruges

Romantic, family-owned hotel in a delightful setting and with luxurious antique furnishings.

P.145 ▸ ACCOMMODATION

▼ Adornes, Bruges

Excellent hotel in a handsome setting and with a sleek, modern interior.

P.144 ▸ ACCOMMODATION

▼ Boatel, Ghent

This former canal barge has been turned into one of Ghent's most appealing hotels.

P.147 ▸ ACCOMMODATION

▲ Relais Oud Huis Amsterdam, Bruges

Classic eighteenth-century mansion sympathetically converted into a four-star hotel.

P.145 ▸ ACCOMMODATION

Historic hotels

Bruges, and to a lesser extent Ghent, possess a hatful of historic hotels. Some occupy grand nineteenth-century mansions; others occupy antique brick houses; while yet others are set in former monasteries and convents. All provide extremely comfortable lodgings in a style that matches their environs.

▼ Jacobs, Bruges

Appealing and reasonably priced hotel in a pleasingly modernized old brick building.

P.144 ▶ ACCOMMODATION

▲ De Goczoput, Bruges

Occupying a former convent, this outstanding hotel is one of the best bargains in town.

P.144 ▸ ACCOMMODATION

▼ Monasterium Poortaokere, Ghent

The most unusual hotel in Ghent, set in a tidily converted nineteenth-century monastery.

P.147 ▸ ACCOMMODATION

▲ Walburg, Bruges

Well-appointed hotel in a handsome nineteenth-century mansion.

P.145 ▸ ACCOMMODATION

Hostels

Bruges is well equipped with hostels, including an official HI hostel tucked away on the outskirts of town plus several privately run hostels in the centre. All offer inexpensive – if rather spartan – accommodation, either in double rooms or in dormitory beds, and the best also have lively bars and a youthful, friendly atmosphere, making them good places to meet other travellers. Ghent, on the other hand, has just one hostel – but it's a well-kept place right in the city centre.

▲ Passage, Bruges

Arguably the most comfortable and atmospheric hostel in Bruges – and excellent value too.

P.146 ▶ ACCOMMODATION

▲ Charlie Rockets, Bruges

A handy setting near the Markt and a boisterous crew make this a popular hostel.

▶ Bauhaus, Bruges

Well-established hostel with a laidback atmosphere and some of the cheapest rooms in the city.

▼ Jeugdherberg De Draecke, Ghent

Excellent, well-equipped HI-affiliated youth hostel in the city centre.

Flemish food

Flemish food is characteristically straightforward and hearty. Pork, beef, game, fish and seafood, especially mussels, herring and eels, remain the staple items, often cooked with butter, cream and herbs, or sometimes beer. Soup is also common, hearty stew-like affairs mostly offered in a huge tureen from which you can help yourself – a satisfying and reasonably priced meal in itself.

▲ Haring

The Flemings love their herring – preferably (raw) fillets with onions in a bread roll. The *De Visscherie* serves the fanciest herring starters in town.

P.81 ▶ SOUTH OF THE MARKT

▼ Waterzooi

A delicious and filling soup-cum-stew, which is served with either chicken (van kip) or fish (van riviervis). The *Den Dyver* restaurant does a fine line in waterzooi.

P.80 ▸ SOUTH OF THE MARKT

▲ Mussels and chips

If Belgium has a national dish it's mussels (mosselen) and chips, the mussels served up in giant tureens. Try them at *L'intermède*.

P.80 ▸ SOUTH OF THE MARKT

▼ Stoofvlees

Cubes of beef marinated in beer and cooked with herbs and onions – a delicious combination. The *Cafedraal* often has stoofvlees on the menu.

P.88 ▸ SOUTH OF THE MARKT

Restaurants

Bruges and Ghent boast a huge number of restaurants, ranging from deluxe establishments where you can sample exquisite Flemish and French cuisine, through to rudimentary, tourist-orientated places serving up filling meals at bargain-basement prices. Mercifully, very few are owned by chains and consequently the vast majority are small and cosy, with the chef – or chef-owner – hovering around to make sure everything is up to scratch.

▲ Den Dyver

Formal, long-established restaurant specializing in Flemish dishes cooked in beer.

P.80 ▶ SOUTH OF THE MARKT, BRUGES

▲ In Den Wittekop

Friendly, family-run restaurant, serving up all the Flemish classics to a smooth jazz soundtrack.

P.102 ▶ NORTH AND EAST OF THE MARKT, BRUGES

▲ Het Dagelijks Brood

Smashing little café-cum-restaurant with a fine line in breads and soups.

P.63 ▸ THE BURG, BRUGES

▼ Cafedraal

Chic restaurant offering a wide range of French and Flemish dishes.

P.80 ▸ SOUTH OF THE MARKT, BRUGES

Belgian beer

There are about 700 Belgian beers to choose from, and the range is simply mind boggling: there are red beers and brown beers, fruit beers and wheat beers, not to mention super-strong Trappist beers and tart Lambic beers fermented with wild yeast. Most bars in both Bruges and Ghent have a beer menu and, although it's unlikely that any one establishment will have all those listed here, most should have at least a couple.

▲ Kwak

This sweet amber ale is served in distinctive hourglasses placed in a wooden stand.

▲ Gueuze

Double fermented beer with a tart flavour and yellow colour.

▲ Orval

Strong, amber ale produced in an abbey in the south of Belgium.

▼ Kriek

Delightfully refreshing brew, flavoured with cherries (or cherry juice).

▲ Chimay

World–famous brew made by Trappist monks. Try the red top (7%), or the leg-liquefying blue (9%).

Bars

In both Bruges and Ghent drinking can be a delight. Bars run the gamut from traditional, neighbourhood haunts with nicotine-stained walls to sleek modern places and the Euro-style pavement cafés which flank the main squares – the Markt in Bruges and both the Vrijdagmarkt and the Korenmarkt in Ghent.

▲ Wijnbar Est

Infinitely agreeable café-bar offering tasty snacks and light meals washed down with the city's widest selection of wines.

P.82 ▸ SOUTH OF THE MARKT, BRUGES

▲ De Republiek

Fashionably cool and youthful bar with a substantial beer menu.

P.102 ▶ NORTH AND EAST OF THE MARKT, BRUGES

▲ Oud Vlissinghe

Eccentric old bar with oodles of wood panelling, long wooden tables and a pleasant beer garden.

P.102 ▶ NORTH AND EAST OF THE MARKT, BRUGES

▶ De Garre

With an enterprising beer menu and jazzy background music, this is one of the city's most enjoyable bars.

P.56 ▶ THE MARKT, BRUGES

Shopping in Bruges: food and drink

With so much space dedicated to tourism, regular shopping for food and drink plays second fiddle in central Bruges, but there are a string of places devoted to Belgium's gastronomic obsessions: beer and chocolate. With chocolate, it's worth remembering that you really do pay for what you get: the cheaper the product, the more likely it is to have a greater percentage of sugar.

▼ Jenever

The Belgians have a penchant for jenever (Dutch gin); the Bottleshop has a wide variety.

P.53 ▶ THE MARKT, BRUGES

▲ Chocolate Line

Most chocolate shops in Bruges are chains, but this one isn't – and the chocolates are all the better for it.

P.77 ▸ SOUTH OF THE MARKT, BRUGES

▲ Deldycke

The best delicatessan in town, perfect for preparing a picnic.

P.53 ▸ THE MARKT, BRUGES

▼ Bottleshop

There are several hundred different types of Belgian beer and this cheerful shop stocks most of them.

P.53 ▸ THE MARKT, BRUGES

Clothes and fashion

When it comes to clothes and fashion, Bruges and Ghent are minor league, but each of them does have a handful of designer shops where you can pick up some great and very varied gear: Belgium has a lively fashion scene, and its leading designers – like Olivier Strelli – have an international reputation.

▲ Knapp Targa

Arguably the best clothes shop in town, with a wide range of chic clothes, from classic labels to more adventurous styles.

P.77 ▶ SOUTH OF THE MARKT, BRUGES

▲ Rex Spirou

Adventurous designer fashions for the under 30s, plus plenty of accessories.

P.54 ▸ THE MARKT, BRUGES

▼ Quicke

The best shoe shop in Bruges, showcasing top European designers.

P.78 ▸ SOUTH OF THE MARKT, BRUGES

▲ Olivier Strelli

Belgium's most famous clothes designer, known for his simple but modern and elegantly tailored designs for both men and women.

P.54 ▸ THE MARKT, BRUGES &
P.125 ▸ CENTRAL GHENT

Festivals

Bruges, and to a lesser extent Ghent, put on an ambitious programme of festivals and special events. One or two, like the solemn Heilig-Bloedprocessie, are deeply embedded in Flemish history, while others are geared up for the inhabitants of the small surrounding villages. The majority, however – especially the performing arts and film festivals – are primarily aimed at the region's many visitors.

▲ Gentse Feesten

The Ghent Festival is a ten–day party with bands and buskers and an outdoor market, plus lashings of alcohol.

P.42 ▶ ESSENTIALS

▼ Meifoor

From late April to late May, the locals warm up at this annual fun fair.

P.43 ▸ ESSENTIALS

▼ Kerstmarkt

Bruges's Christmas market is a picturesque affair with open–air stalls and a skating rink.

P.43 ▸ ESSENTIALS

▲ Heilig Bloedprocessie

On Ascension Day, the Procession of the Holy Blood celebrates Bruges's holiest icon, a phial holding drops of Christ's blood.

P.43 ▸ ESSENTIALS

Places

The Markt

Passing through Bruges in 1820, William Wordsworth declared that this was where he discovered "a deeper peace than in deserts found". He was neither the first nor the last Victorian to fall in love with the place and by the 1840s there was a substantial British colony here, its members captured and enraptured by the city's medieval architecture and air of lost splendour. Civil service and army pensions went much further in Bruges than back home and the expatriates were not slow to exercise their economic muscle, applying an architectural Gothic Revival brush to parts of the city that weren't "medieval" enough. Time and again, they intervened in municipal planning decisions, allying themselves to like-minded Flemings in a movement which changed, or at least modified, the face of the city – and ultimately paid out megabucks with the arrival of mass tourism in the 1960s.

Thus, Bruges is not the perfectly preserved medieval city described by much tourist literature, but rather a clever, frequently seamless combination of medieval original and nineteenth- and sometimes twentieth-century additions. This is especially true of the city centre and its principal square, the Markt, an airy open space overlooked by the mighty Belfort and flanked on its other three sides by rows of gabled buildings, with horse-drawn buggies clattering over the cobbles between. The biscuit-tin buildings flanking most of the square form a charming ensemble, largely mellow ruddy-brown brick, each gable compatible with but slightly different from its neighbour. The majority are late nineteenth- or twentieth-century recreations – or reinventions – of older buildings, though the former Post Office, which hogs the east side of the square, is a thunderous neo-Gothic edifice which refuses to camouflage its more modern construction.

The Monument to Pieter de Coninck and Jan Breydel

The burghers of nineteenth-century Bruges were keen to put something suitably civic in the middle of the Markt and the result is the

A **combined ticket** for any five of Bruges' fourteen municipal museums – including the Stadhuis, Belfort, Renaissancezaal 't Brugse Vrije, Arentshuis, and the Groeninge, Gruuthuse and Memling museums – costs €15 and can be bought at any of the fourteen featured places, as well as from the tourist office. Depending on exactly which museums you visit, the ticket can offer a significant saving compared to buying individual tickets. Note that, with the exception of the Stadhuis, the Belfort and the Renaissancezaal 't Brugse Vrije, all these museums are closed on Mondays.

THE MARKT

Biekorf &
Bibliotheek

EIER-
MARKT

MUNT
PLEIN

Café
Craenenburg

MARKT

ST-AMANDSSTRAAT

GELDMUNTSTRAAT

KORTE
ZILVERSTRAAT

KLEINE ST
AMANDSSTRAAT

KOPSTRAAT

STEENSTRAAT

ST NIKLAASSTRAAT

OUDE BURG

Bus Stop

BREIDELSTRAAT

Hallen
&
Belfort

HALLESTRAAT

WOLLESTRAAT

BURG

N

0   100 m

SHOPS

The Bottle Shop	h	Oil & Vinegar	c
Callebert	o	Olivier Strelli (for men)	d
Deldycke	n	Olivier Strelli	
Diksmuids		(for women)	b
boterhuis	e	Reisboekhandel	f
INNO	m	Rex Spirou	a
Javana	k	De Reyghere	g
La Pasta	j	TinTin Shop	i

RESTAURANTS

Den Amand	3
De Stove	4

BAR

De Garre	5

CAFÉS

De Belegde Boterham	6
Café Craenenburg	2
Café de Medici	1

conspicuous monument to
Pieter de Coninck, of the guild
of weavers, and Jan Breydel,
dean of the guild of butchers.
Standing close together, they
clutch the hilt of the same
sword, their faces turned to the
south in slightly absurd poses
of heroic determination – a
far cry from the gory events
which first made them local
heroes. At dawn on Friday,
May 18, 1302, in what was
later called the Bruges Matins,
their force of rebellious
Flemings crept into the city
and massacred the unsuspecting
French garrison, putting to the
sword anyone who couldn't
correctly pronounce the
Flemish shibboleth *schild en
vriend* ("shield and friend").
Later the same year, the two
guildsmen went on to lead
the city's contingent in the
Flemish army that defeated
the French at the Battle of the
Golden Spurs – no surprise,

then, that the monument takes
its cue from the battle rather
than the massacre. Interestingly
enough, the statue was actually
unveiled twice. In July 1887 a
local committee pulled back
the drapes to celebrate Coninck
and Breydel as Flemings,
whilst in August the city
council organized an official
opening, when King Leopold II
honoured them as Belgians.

The Café Craenenburg

Occupying a relatively
undistinguished modern
building on the corner of
St-Amandsstraat, the *Craenenburg
Café* marks the site of the
eponymous medieval mansion in
which the guildsmen of Bruges
imprisoned the Habsburg heir,
Archduke Maximilian, for three
months in 1488. The reason
for their difference of opinion
was the archduke's efforts to
limit the city's privileges, but
whatever the justice of their

▲ THE MARKT

cause, the guildsmen made a big mistake. Maximilian made all sorts of promises to escape their clutches, but a few weeks after his release his father, Emperor Frederick III, turned up with an army to take imperial revenge, with a bit of hanging here and a bit of burning there. Maximilian became emperor in 1493 and never forgave Bruges, not only failing to honour his promises but also doing his considerable best to push trade north to its great rival, Antwerp.

Outside the Belfort

Filling out the south side of the Markt, but entered via the Hallen (see p.52), the domineering Belfort (belfry) is a potent symbol of civic pride and municipal independence, its distinctive octagonal lantern visible for miles across the surrounding polders. The Belfort was begun in the thirteenth century, when the town was at its richest and most extravagant, but it has had a blighted history. The original wooden version was struck by lightning and burned to the ground in 1280. The present brick replacement, with blind arcading, turrets and towers, was constructed in its place, receiving its octagonal stone lantern and a second

wooden spire in the 1480s, though the new spire was lost to a thunderstorm a few years later. Undeterred, the Flemings promptly added a third spire, though when this went up in smoke in 1741 the locals gave up, settling for the present structure with the addition of a stone parapet in 1822. It's a pity they didn't have another go, if only to sabotage Longfellow's metre in his dire but oft-quoted poem *The Belfry of Bruges*: "In the market place of Bruges/Stands the Belfry old and brown/Thrice consumed and thrice rebuilt ...", and so

▲ CONINCK AND BREYDEL MONUMENT

▲ THE BELFORT

behind a set of fancy – and still surprisingly well-preserved – iron grilles. Here also is an iron trumpet with which a watchman could warn the town of a fire outbreak – though given the size of the trumpet, it's hard to believe this was very effective.

The Belfort's Carillon Chamber

Carrying on up the staircase, you soon reach the Belfort's Carillon Chamber, where you can observe the slow turning of the large spiked drum that controls the 47 bells of the municipal carillon. The largest bell weighs no less than six tonnes. Like other Flemish cities, bells were first used in Bruges in the fourteenth century as a means of regulating the working day, and as such reflected the development of a wage economy – employers were keen to keep tabs on their employees. Bells also served as a sort of public address system with everyone understanding the signals: pealing bells, for example, announced good news; tolling bells summoned the city to the Markt; and a rapid sequence of bells warned of danger. By the early fifteenth century a short peal of bells marked the hour, and from this developed the carillon (*beiaard*), with Bruges installing its present version in the middle of the eighteenth century. The city still employs a full-time bell-ringer and you're likely to see him fiddling around preparing his concerts in the Carillon Room, a small and intimate little cubby hole right near the top of the belfry. A few stairs up from here you emerge onto the roof of the

on. Few would say the Belfort is good-looking – it's large and really rather clumsy – but it does have a certain ungainly charm, though this was lost on G.K. Chesterton, who described it as "an unnaturally long-necked animal, like a giraffe".

The Hallen, and inside the Belfort

Entry to the Belfort (Tues–Sun 9.30am–5pm, last entry 4.15pm; €5) is via the quadrangular Hallen at its base. Now used for temporary exhibitions, the Hallen is a much-restored edifice dating from the thirteenth century. In the middle, overlooked by a long line of galleries, is a rectangular courtyard, which originally served as the town's principal market, its cobblestones once crammed with merchants and their wares. On the north side of the courtyard, up a flight of steps, is the belfry entrance.

Inside, the belfry staircase begins innocuously, but gets steeper and very much narrower nearer the top. On the way up, it passes several chambers, beginning with the Treasury Room, where the town charters and money chest were locked for safekeeping

Carillon concerts

Carillon concerts, which are audible all over the city centre, are performed from late June to September on Monday, Wednesday and Saturday (9–10pm) and Sunday (2.15–3pm), and from October to mid-June on Wednesday, Saturday and Sunday (2.15–3pm).

Belfort, which offers fabulous views over the city, especially in the late afternoon, when the warm colours of the town are at their deepest.

Shops

The Bottle Shop

Wollestraat 13 ☎ 050 34 99 80. Daily 10am–7pm. Just off the Markt – so very popular with tourists – this bright and cheerful establishment stocks several hundred types of beer, oodles of whisky and *jenever* (gin), as well as all sorts of special glasses to drink them from – the Belgians have specific glasses for many of their beers.

Callebert

Wollestraat 25 ☎ 050 33 50 61, ⓦ www.callebert.be. Mon 2–6pm, Tues–Sat 10am–noon & 2–6pm, Sun 3–6pm. Bruges's top contemporary homeware, ceramics and furniture store, featuring leading brands such as Alessi and Bodum, as well as less familiar names. They also stock everything from bags, watches and jewellery to household utensils, textiles and tableware, while the shop's art gallery presents the best of contemporary design, primarily in glass and ceramics, along with calligraphy and photography.

Deldycke

Wollestraat 23 ① 050 33 43 35. Daily except Tues 9.30am–6pm. The best delicatessen in town, with helpful service and every treat you can think of – from snails and on up the evolutionary tree – plus pâtés and a good selection of beer.

Diksmuids boterhuis

Geldmuntstraat 23 ☎ 050 33 32 43. Mon–Sat 9.30am–12.30pm & 2–6.30pm. Traditional shop

▼ THE CARILLON CHAMBER

specializing in cooked meats and Belgian cheeses.

INNO

Steenstraat 11–15 ☎050 33 06 03. Mon–Sat 9.15am–6pm. The best department store in town, spread over four floors and selling everything from high-quality clothes and perfumes through to leather goods, underwear, household utensils and jewellery.

Javana

Steenstraat 6 ☎050 33 36 05, ⊛www .javana.be. Mon–Sat 9am–6pm. Javana has been selling the best coffees and teas in the world from these neat little premises for over fifty years, and also stocks the full range of accessories for coffee- and tea-making.

La Pasta

Kleine St-Amandsstraat 12 ☎050 34 23 01. Tues–Fri 9.30am–1pm & 2–6pm, Sat 9.30am–6pm. Popular with locals and visitors alike, this cosy, family-run food shop sells everything Italian, its speciality being delicious ready-cooked meals. Also stocks a good range of Italian and French wines.

Oil & Vinegar

Geldmuntstraat 11 ☎050 34 56 50, ⊛www.oilvinegar.com. Mon–Sat 10am–6pm. Mediterranean gift-shop-cum-foodstore offering an assortment of sauces, mustards and cooking oils in attractive jars and glass bottles, plus a good range of Tuscan cookbooks.

Olivier Strelli (for men)

Geldmuntstraat 19 ☎050 33 26 75, ⊛www.strelli.be. Mon–Sat 10am–6.30pm. Men's branch of Belgium's well-known designer selling expensive, top-of-the-range contemporary tailored designs with a touch of individuality; the fitted shirts and soft woollens with characteristic diagonal zips are particularly popular.

Olivier Strelli (for women)

Eiermarkt 3 ☎050 34 38 37, ⊛www .strelli.be. Mon–Sat 10am–6.30pm. One of Belgium's most established designers, Strelli has been creating simple but modern clothes for years. His designs include tailored trousers and fitted jackets, often in muted tones with the odd splash of colour thrown in. Pricey.

Reisboekhandel

Markt 13 ☎050 49 12 29, ⊛www .dereyghere.be. Mon–Sat 9.30am–12.30pm & 1.30–6pm. Specialist travel branch of the adjacent De Reyghere (see below), with a wide selection of travel guides, some in English, plus road and city maps and hiking and cycling maps of the surrounding areas. Also stocks travel-related English–language magazines.

Rex Spirou

Geldmuntstraat 18 ☎050 34 66 50, ⊛www.rex-spirou.com. Mon–Sat 9.30am–6.30pm. Chic and sharp designer clothes for the young and cool – or at least the self-conscious – plus a good line in accessories, from jewellery to bags and belts.

De Reyghere

Markt 12 ☎050 33 34 03, ⊛www .dereyghere.be. Mon–Sat 8.30am–6.15pm. Founded over one hundred years ago, De Reyghere is something of a local institution and a meeting place for every book-lover in town. The shop stocks a wide range of domestic and foreign literature, art and gardening books and travel guides, and is also good for international newspapers, magazines and periodicals.

TinTin Shop

Steenstraat 3 ☎ 050 33 42 92, ⓦ www.tintinshopbrugge.be. Mon–Sat 9.30am–6pm, Sun 11am–6pm; Oct–March closed Wed. Souvenir-cum-comic shop cashing in on Hergé's quiffed hero, with all sorts of Tintin tackle from T-shirts to comics.

Cafés

De Belegde Boterham

Kleine St Amandsstraat 5. Mon–Sat noon–4pm. Most of the cafés in and around the Markt are firmly tourist-oriented, but this bright and breezy little place, in attractively renovated old premises, has a local following on account of its fresh sandwiches (€7–10) and tasty salads (€10–12).

Café Craenenburg

Markt 16. Daily 10am till late. Unlike the other touristy cafés lining up along the Markt, this old-fashioned place still attracts a loyal, local clientele. With its leather- and wood-panelling, wooden benches and mullion windows, the *Craenenburg* has the flavour of old Flanders, and although the daytime-only food is routine, it has a good range of beers, including a locally produced, tangy brown ale called Brugse Tripel.

Café de Medici

Geldmuntstraat 9. Mon–Sat 9am–6pm. An enjoyable antidote to the plain modernism of many of its rivals, this attractive café boasts an extravagantly ornate interior, complete with huge mirror and spindly curving staircase. It also has the best range of coffees in town, not to mention mouthwatering cakes and tarts, plus sandwiches and salads too.

Restaurants

Den Amand

St Amandsstraat 4 ☎ 050 34 01 22. Mon, Tues & Thurs–Sat noon–3pm & 6–10pm, Sun 6–10pm. Decorated in pleasant modern style, this

▼ CAFÉ CRAENENBURG

▲ DE GARRE

cosy and informal family-run restaurant offers inventive cuisine combining French and Flemish traditions. Mains from the limited but well-chosen menu – featuring dishes such as swordfish in seafood jus and seafood *waterzooi* (soup) – average a very reasonable €20. It's a small place, so best to book a few hours in advance.

De Stove

Kleine St Amandsstraat 4 ☎ 050 33 78 35. Mon, Tues, Sat & Sun noon–1.45pm & 6.45–9.30pm, Fri 6.45–9.30pm. Small and extraordinarily cosy Franco-Belgian restaurant that's recommended by just about everyone, including Michelin. The menu is carefully constructed, with fish and meat dishes given equal prominence. Mains €22–25, set three-course menus €44, or €60 with wine. Reservations essential.

Bars

De Garre

De Garre 1. Mon-Fri noon–midnight, Sat & Sun 5pm–1am. Down a narrow alley off Breidelstraat, between the Markt and the Burg, this cramped but charming tavern (*estaminet*) has an outstanding range of Belgian beers and tasty snacks with classical music adding to the relaxed air.

The Burg

From the east side of the Markt, Breidelstraat leads through to the city's other main square, the Burg, named after the fortress built here by the first count of Flanders, Baldwin Iron Arm, in the ninth century. The fortress disappeared centuries ago, but the Burg long remained the centre of political and ecclesiastical power, with the Stadhuis (Town Hall) – which has survived – on one side, and St Donatian's Cathedral – which hasn't – on the other. Fringing the southern half of the Burg is the city's finest architectural ensemble, an especially handsome mix of late-Gothic and Renaissance buildings including the Stadhuis and the Basilica of the Holy Blood.

Heilig Bloed Basiliek (Basilica of the Holy Blood)

April–Sept daily 9.30am–noon & 2–6pm; Oct–March Mon–Tues & Thurs–Sun 10am–noon & 2–4pm, Wed 10am–noon; free. The city's most important shrine, the Heilig Bloed Basiliek is named after the holy relic that found its way here in the Middle Ages. The basilica divides into two parts. Tucked away in the corner is the lower chapel, a shadowy crypt-like affair, originally built at the start of the twelfth century to shelter another relic, a piece of St Basil, one of the great figures of the early Greek Church. The chapel's heavy and simple Romanesque lines are decorated with just one relief, carved above an interior doorway and showing the baptism of Basil, in which a strange giant bird, representing the Holy Spirit, plunges into a pool of water.

The upper chapel, next door up a curving, low-vaulted staircase, was built just a few years later but has been renovated so frequently that it's impossible to make out

the original structure; it also suffers from excessively rich nineteenth-century decoration. The chapel itself may be disappointing, but the large silver tabernacle that holds the

▲ HEILIG BLOED BASILIEK

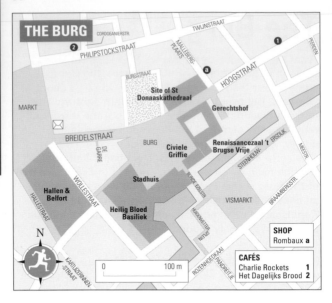

THE BURG

CORDOEANIERSTR.

TWIJNSTRAAT

PHILIPSTOCKSTRAAT

MALLEBERGPLAATS

HOOGSTRAAT

BURGSTRAAT

MARKT

Site of St
Donaaskathedraal

Gerechtshof

BREIDELSTRAAT

BURG

Civiele
Griffie

Renaissancezaal 't
Brugse Vrije

DE GARRE

Stadhuis

Hallen &
Belfort

Heilig Bloed
Basiliek

VISMARKT

HALLESTRAAT

WOLLESTRAAT

BLINDE EZELSTR.

HUIDENVETTERS

STEENHOUW.

ERSDIJK

MEESTR.

BRAAMBERGSTR.

N

KARTUIZERINNEN
STRAAT

ROZENHOEDKAAI

PANDREITJE

0   100 m

SHOP
Rombaux a

CAFÉS
Charlie Rockets 1
Het Dagelijks Brood 2

rock-crystal phial of the Holy
Blood is simply magnificent,
being the gift of Albert and
Isabella of Spain in 1611. The
Habsburg King Philip II of
Spain had granted control of
the Spanish Netherlands (now
Belgium) to his daughter
Isabella and her husband
Albert in 1598, but they were
imprudent rulers, continuing
the long-winded war against
the Protestant Dutch to the
north without success and
exalting the Catholic faith
– as per the tabernacle – whilst
simultaneously persecuting those
Protestants who remained in
their fiefdom.

The phial itself (see box
opposite) was one of the holiest
relics in medieval Europe,
purporting to contain a few
drops of blood and water washed
from the body of Christ by
Joseph of Arimathea. The Holy
Blood is still venerated and,
despite modern scepticism,
reverence for it remains strong,

not least on Ascension Day
(mid-May) when it is carried
through the town in the Heilig-
Bloedprocessie (Procession
of the Holy Blood, see box
opposite). The reliquary that
holds the phial during the
procession is displayed in the
tiny treasury (same times as
basilica; €1.50), next to the
upper chapel. Dating from 1617,
the reliquary is a superb piece
of work, the gold-and-silver
superstructure encrusted with
jewels and decorated with tiny
religious scenes. The treasury
also contains an incidental
collection of vestments and lesser
reliquaries plus a handful of late
medieval paintings, most notably
a finely executed triptych of the
Deposition by Gerard David
(1460–1523) and a naïve panel-
painting entitled *Scenes from the
Life of St Barbara* by the Master
of the St Barbara Legend. The
tower in which the saint's father
imprisoned her on account
of her Christian faith became

The Holy Blood

Local legend asserts that the **Heilig Bloed** (Holy Blood) was the gift of Diederik d'Alsace, a Flemish knight who distinguished himself by his bravery during the Second Crusade and was given the phial by a grateful patriarch of Jerusalem in 1150. It is, however, rather more likely that the relic was acquired during the sacking of Constantinople in 1204, when the crusaders ignored their collective job description and, instead of ridding Palestine of its Moslem rulers, simply slaughtered the Byzantines instead – hence the historical invention involving Diederik. Whatever the truth, after several weeks in Bruges the relic was found to be dry, but thereafter the dried blood proceeded to liquefy every Friday at 6pm until 1325, a miracle attested to by all sorts of church dignitaries, including Pope Clement V.

The failure, in 1325, of the Holy Blood to liquefy prompted all sorts of conjecture – did it mean that Bruges had lost favour in the eyes of God? – but the phial, or more exactly its dried contents, remain an object of veneration even today, not least on Ascension Day (mid-May), when it is carried through the town in a colourful but solemn procession, the **Heilig-Bloedprocessie** (Procession of the Holy Blood). The procession starts on 't Zand in front of the new Concertgebouw (Concert Hall) at 3pm and then wends its way round the centre taking in Steenstraat, Simon Stevinplein, Dyver, Wollestraat, the Markt, Geldmuntstraat and Noordzandstraat before regaining 't Zand at about 5.30pm. Grandstand tickets (€5–11) are sold at the main tourist office (see p.155) from March 1.

Barbara's symbol and is shown here under construction. Look out also, in the glass cabinet between the windows, for Mary of Burgundy's dinky little crown and, above the treasury door, for the faded strands of a locally woven seventeenth-century tapestry depicting St Augustine's funeral, the sea of helmeted heads, torches and pikes that surround the monks and abbots very much a Catholic view of a muscular State supporting a holy Church.

The Stadhuis (Town Hall)

Daily 9.30am–5pm; €2.50 including the Renaissancezaal 't Brugse Vrije (see p.61). Immediately to the left of the basilica, the Stadhuis has a beautiful sandstone facade of 1376, though its statues, mostly of the counts and countesses of Flanders, are modern replacements for those destroyed by the occupying French army in 1792. Inside, the impressive, high-ceilinged **entrance hall** makes a suitably grand home for a collection of ambitious nineteenth-century paintings, either romantic

▼ THE STADHUIS

reworkings of the city's history designed to reassure the council of its distinguished pedigree, or didactic canvases to keep it up to the mark. The paintings on display are changed regularly, but perhaps the most original is the dramatic *Death of Mary of Burgundy* by Camille van Camp (1834–91), depicting the hunting accident which polished the young queen off in 1482. There's also a curious painting showing a certain Baron de Croeser welcoming Napoleon to the Stadhuis; the baron wears a forced smile – not surprisingly, given that the emperor was about to sweep away the ancient privileges that had sustained the city's oligarchs. There's also a large portrait of the empress Maria Theresa decked out in the amazing lace dress she had made for her in Flanders in 1744: she obviously felt it suited her – witness the haughty pose and the dainty foot poking out from under the hem.

▼ THE GOTHIC HALL

Upstairs, the magnificent **Gothic Hall** of 1400 has been restored in style, its ceiling a vibrant mixture of maroon, dark brown, black and gold, dripping pendant arches like decorated stalactites. The ribs of the arches converge in twelve circular vault-keys, showing scenes from the New Testament, though they're hard to see without binoculars. Down below – and much easier to view – are the sixteen fancy gilded corbels which support them. These represent the months and the four elements, beginning in the left-hand corner beside the chimney with January (inscribed "Winter") and continuing clockwise right round the hall; the gilded chariots of Air and Earth follow June ("Lentemaand"), Fire and Water come after September ("Herfst"). The wall frescoes were commissioned in 1895 to illustrate the history of the town – or rather history as the council wanted to recall it. The largest scene, commemorating the victory over the French at the Battle of the Golden Spurs in 1302, has lots of noble knights hurrahing, though it's hard to take this seriously when you look at the dogs, one of which clearly has a mismatch between its body and head.

Next door to the Gothic Hall is the **Historische zaal** (Historical Room), where a routine display of miscellaneous municipal artefacts is partly redeemed by two finely drawn, sixteenth-century city maps.

The Civiele Griffie and the Renaissancezaal 't Brugse Vrije

Next door to the Stadhuis, above and beside the archway spanning Blinde Ezelstraat

(Blind Donkey Street), is the bright and cheery **Civiele Griffie** (Records Office; not open to the public), which was built to house the municipal records office in 1537, its elegant facade decorated with Renaissance columns and friezes superimposed on the Gothic lines of the gable below.

The adjacent **Paleis van het Brugse Vrije** (Mansion of the Liberty of Bruges) is demure by comparison, but nonetheless boasts a distinguished history. Established in the Middle Ages, the Liberty of Bruges was a territorial subdivision of Flanders which enjoyed extensive delegated powers, controlling its own finances and judiciary. Power was exercised by a council of aldermen and it was they who demolished most of the original Gothic

building in the early eighteenth century – before Napoleon abolished them. Today the building is home to the city archives, but pop inside to look at the Schepenkamer (Aldermen's Room), the sole survivor from the fifteenth-century mansion and now known as the **Renaissancezaal 't Brugse Vrije** (Renaissance Hall of the Liberty of Bruges; daily 9.30am–12.30pm & 1.30–5pm; €2.50 including the Stadhuis). Dominating the room is an enormous marble and oak chimneypiece, a superb example of Renaissance carving completed in 1531 to celebrate the defeat of the French at Pavia six years earlier and the advantageous Treaty of Cambrai that followed. A paean of praise to the Habsburgs, the work features the Emperor Charles V

Charles the Good and Galbert of Bruges

In 1127, St Donaaskathedraal witnessed an event that shocked the whole of Bruges, when the Count of Flanders, **Charles the Good**, was murdered while he was at prayer in the choir. A gifted and far-sighted ruler, Charles eschewed foreign entanglements in favour of domestic matters – unlike most of his predecessors – and improved the lot of the poor by trying to ensure a regular supply of food and controlling prices in times of shortage. These far-sighted policies, along with his personal piety, earned Charles his sobriquet, but the count's attempts to curb his leading vassals brought him into conflict with the powerful Erembald clan. The Erembalds had no intention of submitting to Charles, so they assassinated him and took control of the city. Their success was, however, short-lived. Supporters of Charles rallied and the murderers took refuge in the tower of St Donatian's, from where they were winkled out and promptly dispatched.

Shocked by the murder, one of Charles's clerks, a certain **Galbert of Bruges**, decided to write a detailed journal of the events that led up to the assassination and the bloody chaos that ensued. Unlike other contemporary source materials, the journal had no sponsor, which makes it a uniquely honest account of events, admittedly from the perspective of the count's entourage, with Galbert criticizing many of the city's leading figures, clergy and nobles alike. Galbert's journal provides a fascinating insight into twelfth-century Bruges and it's well written too (in a wordy sort of way) – as in the account of Charles' death: "when the count was praying … then at last, after so many plans and oaths and pacts among themselves, those wretched traitors … slew the count, who was struck down with swords and run through again and again". The full text is reprinted in *The Murder of Charles the Good*, edited by James Bruce Ross.

▲ CIVIELE GRIFFIE

and his Austrian and Spanish relatives, each person identified by the free audio guide, though it's the trio of bulbous codpieces that really catch the eye. The alabaster frieze running below the carvings was a caution for the Liberty's magistrates, who held their courts here. In four panels, it relates the then familiar Biblical story of Susanna, in which – in the first panel – two old men surprise her bathing in her garden and threaten to accuse her of adultery if she resists their advances. Susanna does just that and the second panel shows her in court. In the third panel, Susanna is about to be put to death, but the magistrate, Daniel, interrogates the two men and uncovers their perjury. Susanna is acquitted and, in the final scene, the two men are stoned to death.

The site of St Donaaskathedraal

Adjoining the Paleis van het Brugse Vrije is the plodding courtyard complex of the Gerechtshof (Law Courts), dating from 1722 and now home to municipal offices.

Beyond, in the northeast corner of the Burg, the modern *Crowne Plaza* hotel marks the site of St Donaaskathedraal (St Donatian's Cathedral), which was razed by the French army of occupation in 1799. This splendid structure boasted an octagonal main building flanked by a sixteen-sided ambulatory topped off by an imposing tower. The foundations were uncovered in 1955 but were then promptly reinterred and, although there are vague plans to carry out another archeological dig, nothing has happened yet.

The curious Toyo Ito pavilion across from the hotel is probably the city's most unsuccessful piece of modern art, known locally – for reasons that are obvious as soon as you see it – as the "car wash". Rumour has it that it will soon be removed.

Shops

Rombaux
Mallebergplaats 13 ☎ 050 33 25 75. Mon 2–6.30pm, Tues–Fri 9am–12.30pm & 2–6.30pm, Sat

10am–6pm. The idiosyncratic facade of faded old album covers conceals all manner of musical goodies, including classical to modern CDs (with a particularly good selection of jazz and blues), plus vinyl and sheet music.

Cafés

Charlie Rockets

Hoogstraat 19–21 ☎050 49 00 75, 🕸www.charlierockets.com. Daily noon–2.30pm & 6–10.30pm. In the same building as the eponymous hostel (see p.146), this American-style café-bar – or at least an approximation of it – attracts a youthful clientele and serves reasonably priced Italian food. There's also a large adjoining pool room with five tables and live music every fortnight or so.

Het Dagelijks Brood

Philipstockstraat 21. Daily except Tues 8am–6pm. This excellent bread shop doubles as a wholefood café with one long wooden table – enforced communalism, which can be good fun – and a few smaller side tables too. The home-made soup and bread makes a meal in itself for just €8, or you can chomp away on a range of snacks and cakes.

South of the Markt

The bustling area to the south of the Markt holds the city's busiest shopping streets as well as many of its key buildings and most important museums. The area is at its prettiest among the old lanes near the cathedral, Salvatorskathedraal, which lays claim to be the city's most satisfying church, though the Onze Lieve Vrouwekerk, just to the south, comes a close second. There is more cuteness in the huddle of whitewashed cottages of the Begijnhof and at the adjacent Minnewater, the so – called "Lake of Love". As for the museums, St Janshospitaal offers the exquimedieval paintings of Hans Memling, the Gruuthuse is strong on applied art, especially tapestries and antique furniture, and the Groeninge (p.83) holds a wonderful sample of early Flemish art.

The Vismarkt and Huidenvettersplein

From the arch beside the Stadhuis on the Burg, Blinde Ezelstraat (Blind Donkey Street) leads south across the canal to the plain and sombre, eighteenth-century Doric colonnades of the **Vismarkt** (fish market), though, with its handful of fish traders, this is but a shadow of its former self. Neither are there any tanners in the huddle of

picturesque houses that crimp the **Huidenvettersplein**, the square at the centre of the old tanners' quarter immediately to the west – a good job as the locals of yesteryear often complained of the stench. Tourists converge on this pint-sized square in their droves, holing up in its bars and restaurants and snapping away at the postcard-perfect views of the belfry from the adjacent Rozenhoedkaai.

▼ DIJVER CANAL

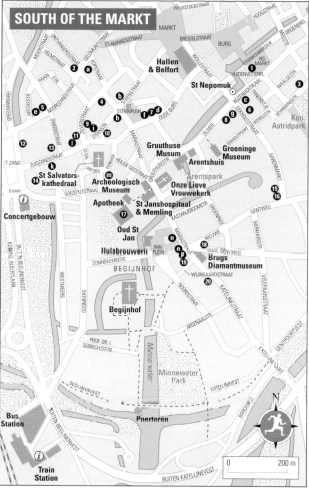

SOUTH OF THE MARKT

SHOPS		CAFÉS		RESTAURANTS	
Bilbo	**e**	De Bron	**20**	Cafedraal	**11**
The Chocolate Line	**h**	Detavernier,		Christophe	**16**
Claeys	**p**	Tearoom Carpe Diem	**19**	Den Dyver	**8**
Classics	**f**	't Eekhoetje	**6**	L'Intermède	**5**
Decorte	**a**	Gran Kaffee de Passage	**13**	Patrick Devos	
Kasimir's Antique		Laurent	**10**	"De Zilveren Pauw"	**9**
Studio	**c**	Lokkedize	**14**	Tanuki	**18**
Knapp Targa	**j**	De Verbeelding	**7**	De Visscherie	**1**
Leonidas	**n**				
Louis Delhaize	**d**	**BARS & CLUBS**			
De Meester	**g**	B-in	**17**		
Neuhaus	**b**	De Bolero	**15**		
Pollentier	**m**	Het Brugs Beertje	**4**		
Quicke	**k**	L'Estaminet	**3**		
Standaard Boekhandel	**i**	Ma Rica Rokk	**12**		
De Striep	**o**	Wijnbar Est	**2**		

▲ ST JOHN NEPOMUK, WOLLESTRAAT

Wollestraat bridge

Just west of Huidenvettersplein is the **Wollestraat bridge**, overlooked by a statue of the patron saint of bridges, St John Nepomuk, a fourteenth-century Bohemian priest who was purportedly thrown bound and gagged into the River Vltava for refusing to reveal the confessional secrets of the queen to her husband, King Wenceslas IV. The bridge marks the start of the Dijver, which tracks along the canal as far as Nieuwstraat, passing the path to the first of the city's main museums, the Groeninge (see p.83), just before reaching the Arentshuis.

The Arentshuis

Dijver 16. Tues–Sun 9.30am–5pm; €3, or free with Groeninge Museum ticket. The Arentshuis occupies a good-looking eighteenth–century mansion with a stately porticoed entrance. Now a museum, the interior is divided into two separate sections: the ground floor is given over to temporary exhibitions, usually of fine art, while the Brangwyn Museum upstairs displays the moody sketches, etchings, lithographs, studies and paintings of the much-travelled artist Sir Frank Brangwyn (1867–1956). Born in Bruges of Welsh parents, Brangwyn flitted between Britain and Belgium, donating this sample of his work to his native town in 1936. Apprenticed to William Morris in the early 1880s and an official UK war artist in World War I, Brangwyn was nothing if not versatile, turning his hand to several different media, though his forceful drawings and sketches are much more appealing than his paintings, which often slide into sentimentality. In particular, look out for the sequence of line drawings exploring industrial themes – powerful, almost melodramatic scenes of shipbuilding, docks, construction and the like. This penchant for dark and gloomy industrial scenes bore little relationship to the British artistic trends of his day and they attracted muted reviews. Better received were his murals, whose bold designs and strong colours attracted almost universal acclaim – and a 1920s commission to turn out a series for Britain's House of Lords. In

▲ BRANGWYN SCULPTURE, ARENTSHUIS

A **combined ticket** for any five of Bruges' fourteen municipal museums – including the Stadhuis, Belfort, Renaissancezaal 't Brugse Vrije, Arentshuis, and the Groeninge, Gruuthuse and Memling museums – costs €15 and can be bought at any of the fourteen featured places, as well as from the tourist office. Depending on exactly which museums you visit, the ticket can offer a significant saving compared to buying individual tickets. Note that, with the exception of the Stadhuis, the Belfort and the Renaissancezaal 't Brugse Vrije, all these museums are closed on Mondays.

the event, these murals, whose theme was the splendour of the British Empire, ended up in Swansea Guildhall, though several of the preparatory sketches are displayed here in the Arentshuis.

The Arentspark

The Arentshuis stands in the north corner of the pocket-sized Arentspark, whose brace of forlorn stone columns are all that remain of the Waterhalle, which once stood on the east side of the Markt. Demolished in 1787, the Waterhalle straddled the most central of the city's canals, with boats sailing inside the building to unload their cargoes. When part of the canal – between Jan van Eyckplein and the Dijver – was covered over in the middle of the eighteenth century, the Waterhalle became redundant

and its place was subsequently taken by the main post office.

Also in the Arentspark is the tiniest of humpbacked bridges – St Bonifaciusbrug – whose stonework is framed against a tumble of antique brick houses. One of Bruges's most picturesque (and photographed) spots, the bridge looks like the epitome of everything medieval, but in fact it was only built in 1910. Next to the far side of the bridge is a pensive, modern statue of Juan Luis Vives, a Spanish Jew and friend of Erasmus, who settled here in the early sixteenth century to avoid persecution. It was a wise decision: back in Spain his family had converted to Christianity, but even that failed to save them. His father was burnt at the stake in 1525 and his dead mother was dug up and her bones burned.

▼ ST BONIFACIUSBRUG

The Gruuthuse Museum

Dijver 17. Tues–Sun 9.30am–5pm;
€6. The Gruuthuse Museum
occupies a rambling mansion
dating from the fifteenth
century, a fine example of civil
Gothic architecture which takes
its name from the houseowners'
historical right to tax the *gruit*,
the dried herb and flower
mixture once added to barley
during the beer-brewing process
to improve the flavour. The last
lord of the *gruit* died in 1492
and, after many twists and turns,
the mansion was eventually
turned into a museum to hold
a hotchpotch of Flemish fine,
applied and decorative arts,
mostly dating from the medieval
and early modern period. The
museum's strongest suit is its
superb collection of tapestries,
mostly woven in Brussels or
Bruges during the sixteenth
and seventeenth centuries,
although its most famous
artefact is a much-reproduced
polychromatic terracotta bust of
a youthful Emperor Charles V.
The house's most unusual
feature is the oak-panelled
oratory that juts out from the
first floor to overlook the altar
of the Onze Lieve Vrouwekerk
next door. A curiously intimate
room, the oratory allowed the
lords of the *gruit* to worship
without leaving home – a real
social coup.

Onze Lieve Vrouwekerk (Church of Our Lady)

Mon–Sat 9.30am–4.50pm, Sun
1.30–4.50pm; free. Next door
to the Gruuthuse, the Onze
Lieve Vrouwekerk is a rambling
shambles of a building, a
clamour of different dates and
styles, whose brick spire is – at
122m – one of the tallest in
Belgium. Entered from the
south, the **nave** was three

▲ GRUUTHUSE MUSEUM

hundred years in the making, an
architecturally discordant affair,
whose thirteenth-century, grey-
stone central aisle is the oldest
part of the church. The central
aisle blends in with the south
aisle, but the later, fourteenth-
century north aisle doesn't mesh
at all – even the columns aren't
aligned. This was the result of
changing fashions, not slapdash
work: the High Gothic north
aisle was intended to be the start
of a complete remodelling of the
church, but the money ran out
before the work was finished.

In the south aisle is the
church's most acclaimed objet
d'art, a delicate marble *Madonna
and Child* by **Michelangelo**.
Purchased by a Bruges
merchant, this was the only
one of Michelangelo's works
to leave Italy during the artist's
lifetime and it had a significant
influence on the painters then
working in Bruges, though
its present setting – beneath
gloomy stone walls and set
within a gaudy Baroque altar
– is unprepossessing.

Michelangelo apart, the most
interesting part of the church
is the **chancel** (€2.50), beyond

The Bruges tapestry industry

Tapestry manufacture in Bruges began in the middle of the fourteenth century. The embryonic industry soon came to be based on a dual system of workshop and outworker, the one using paid employees, the other with workers paid on a piecework basis. From the beginning, the town authorities took a keen interest in the business, ensuring consistency by a rigorous system of quality control. The other side of this interventionist policy was less palatable: wages were kept down and the workers were hardly ever able to accumulate enough capital to buy either their own looms or even the raw materials.

There were two great periods of Bruges tapestry-making, the first from the early fifteenth until the middle of the sixteenth century, the second from the 1580s to the 1790s. Tapestry production was a cross between embroidery and ordinary weaving. It consisted of interlacing a wool weft above and below the strings of a vertical linen "chain", a process similar to weaving. However, the weaver had to stop to change colour, requiring as many shuttles for the weft as he or she had colours, as in embroidery. The appearance of a tapestry was entirely determined by the weft, the design being taken from a painting – or cartoon of a painting – to which the weaver made constant reference. Standard-size tapestries took six months to make and were produced exclusively for the very wealthy. The most famous artists of the day were often involved in the preparatory paintings – Pieter Paul Rubens, Bernard van Orley and David Teniers all had tapestry commissions.

There were only two significant types of tapestry: decorative, principally verdures, showing scenes of foliage in an almost abstract way; and pictorial (the Bruges speciality) – usually variations on the same basic themes, particularly rural life, knights, hunting parties, classical gods and goddesses and religious scenes. Over the centuries, changes in style were strictly limited, though the early part of the seventeenth century saw an increased use of elaborate woven borders, an appreciation of perspective and the use of a far brighter, more varied range of colours.

the black-and-white marble rood screen. Here you'll find the mausoleums of Charles the Bold and his daughter Mary of Burgundy (see box, p.71), two exquisite examples of Renaissance carving, their side panels decorated with coats of arms connected by the most intricate of floral designs. The royal figures are enhanced in the detail, from the helmet and gauntlets placed gracefully by Charles' side to the pair of watchful dogs nestled at Mary's feet. The exploratory hole dug by archeologists beneath the mausoleums during the 1970s (see box, p.71) was never filled in and mirrors now give sight of Mary's coffin along with the burial vaults of several unknown

▲ MICHELANGELO'S MADONNA AND CHILD

medieval dignitaries, three of which have now been moved to the Lanchals Chapel. The coats of arms above the choir stalls are those of the knights of the Order of the Golden Fleece (see box, p.74), who met here in 1468.

Just across the ambulatory from the mausoleums, the **Lanchals Chapel** holds the imposing Baroque gravestone of Pieter Lanchals, a one-time Habsburg official who was executed by the citizens of Bruges in 1488. Legend asserts that he was beheaded for his opposition to Maximilian's temporary imprisonment in the Craenenburg (see p.50) and that, to atone for its crime, Bruges was later obliged to introduce swans to its canals. Both tales are, however, fabrications, seemingly invented in the nineteenth century: Lanchals actually had his head lopped off for being corrupt and was soon forgotten by his erstwhile sponsor, while the swan story seems to have originated with the swan that adorns his

▼ ONZE LIEVE VROUWEKERK, GRAVE FRESCOES

gravestone – the bird was the man's emblem, appropriately enough, as his name means "long neck".

In front of the Lanchals gravestone are three relocated **medieval burial vaults**, each plastered with lime mortar. The inside walls of the vaults sport brightly coloured grave frescoes, a type of art which flourished hereabouts from the late thirteenth to the middle of the fifteenth century. The iconography is fairly consistent, with the long sides mostly bearing one, sometimes two, angels apiece, with most of them shown swinging thuribles (the vessels in which incense is burnt during religious ceremonies). Typically, the short sides show the Crucifixion and the Virgin and Child and there's sometimes an image of the dead person or his/her patron saint too. The background decoration is more varied, with crosses, stars and dots all making appearances as well as two main sorts of flower – roses and bluebells. The frescoes were painted freehand and executed at great speed – Flemings were then buried on the day they died – hence the delightful immediacy of the work.

Sint Janshospitaal

Opposite the entrance to the Onze Lieve Vrouwekerk, the Sint Janshospitaal is a sprawling complex which sheltered the sick of mind and body until well into the nineteenth century. The oldest part – at the front on Mariastraat, behind two church-like gable ends – has been turned into a slick museum (see opposite), whilst the nineteenth-century annexe, reached along a narrow passageway on the north side of the museum,

The earthly remains of Mary of Burgundy and Charles the Bold

The last independent rulers of Flanders were Charles the Bold, the Duke of Burgundy, and his daughter Mary of Burgundy, both of whom died in unfortunate circumstances, Charles during the siege of the French city of Nancy in 1477, Mary after a riding accident in 1482, when she was only 25. Mary was married to Maximilian, a Habsburg prince and future Holy Roman Emperor, who inherited her territories on her death and thus, at a dynastic stroke, Flanders was incorporated into the Habsburg empire.

In the sixteenth century, the Habsburgs relocated to Spain, but they were keen to emphasize their connections with – and historical authority over – Flanders, the richest part of their expanding empire. Nothing did this quite as well as the ceremonial burial – or re-burial – of bits of royal body. Mary was safely ensconced in Bruges' Onze Lieve Vrouwekerk, but the body of Charles was in a makeshift grave in Nancy. Emperor Charles V, the great grandson of Charles the Bold, had – or thought he had – this body exhumed and carried to Bruges, where it was re-interred next to Mary. There were, however, persistent rumours that the French, traditional enemies of the Habsburgs, had deliberately handed over a dud skeleton, specifically one of the knights who died in the same engagement. In the 1970s, archeologists had a bash at solving the mystery. They dug beneath Charles and Mary's mausoleums in the Onze Lieve Vrouwekerk but, amongst the assorted tombs, failed to authoritatively identify either the body or even the tomb of Charles; Mary proved more tractable, with her skeleton confirming the known details of her hunting accident. Buried alongside her was the urn which contained the heart of her son, Philip the Fair, placed here in 1506.

has been converted into an exhibition-cum-shopping centre called – rather confusingly – Oud St-Jan. The passageway also passes the hospital's old Apotheek (apothecary: Tues–Sun 9.30am–5pm; free), which comes complete with rows of antique porcelain, earthenware and glass jars.

The Hospitaalmuseum

Tues–Sun 9.30am–5pm; €8. At the front of the St-Janshospitaal complex, the Hospitaalmuseum divides into two, with one large section – in the former hospital ward – exploring the historical background to the hospital through documents, paintings and religious objets d'art; and a second, smaller section sited in the old hospital chapel which is devoted to six works by Hans Memling (see p.72). In both,

the labelling is minimal, though the audioguide provides copious background information.

Highlights of the larger section include Jan Beerblock's *The Wards of St Janshospitaal* (audioguide no.27; exhibit no.66), a minutely detailed painting of the hospital ward as it was in the late eighteenth century, with patients tucked away in row upon row of tiny, cupboard-like beds. There were 150 beds in total divided into three sections – one for women, one for men and the third for the dying. Other noteworthy paintings include an exquisite Deposition (audioguide no.36; exhibit no.138), a late fifteenth-century version of an original by Rogier van der Weyden, and a stylish, intimately observed diptych (audioguide no.38; exhibit no.153) by Jan Provoost,

▲ ST JANSHOSPITAL MUSEUM

with portraits of Christ and the donor – a friar – on the front and a skull on the back.

The Memling Collection

The former chapel of the Hospitaalmuseum houses six works by **Hans Memling** (1433–94). Born near Frankfurt, Memling spent most of his working life in Bruges, where he was taught by Rogier van der Weyden (see p.84). He adopted much of his tutor's style and stuck to the detailed symbolism of his contemporaries, but his painterly manner was distinctly restrained, often pious and grave. Graceful and warmly coloured, his figures also had a velvet-like quality that greatly appealed to the city's burghers, whose enthusiasm made Memling a rich man – in 1480 he was listed among the town's major moneylenders. Of the six works on display, the most unusual is the *Reliquary of St Ursula*, comprising a miniature wooden Gothic church painted with the story of St Ursula. Six panels show Ursula and her ten companions on their way to Rome, only to be massacred by Huns as they

passed through Germany. It is, however, the mass of incidental detail that makes the reliquary so enchanting – a wonderful evocation of the late medieval world. Equally delightful is the *Mystical Marriage of St Catherine*, the middle panel of a large triptych depicting St Catherine, who represents contemplation, receiving a ring from the baby Jesus to seal their spiritual union. In the background, behind St John, is the giant wooden crane that once dominated the Kraanplein (see p.91).

Memling's skill as a portraitist is demonstrated to exquisite effect in his *Portrait of a Young Woman*, where the richly dressed subject stares dreamily into the middle distance, her hands – in a superb optical illusion – seeming to clasp the picture frame. The lighting is subtle and sensuous, with the woman set against a dark background, her gauze veil dappling the side of her face. A high forehead was then considered a sign of great womanly beauty, so her hair is pulled right back and was probably plucked – as are her eyebrows. There's no knowing who the woman was, but in the seventeenth century her fancy headgear convinced observers that she was one of the legendary Persian sibyls who predicted Christ's birth; so convinced were they that they added the cartouche in the top left hand corner, describing her as Sibylla Sambetha – and the painting is often referred to by this name.

The sixth and final painting, the *Virgin and Martin van Nieuwenhove* diptych is exhibited in the adjoining side chapel. Here, the eponymous merchant has the flush of youth and a hint of arrogance: his lips pout, his hair cascades down to his shoulders and he is dressed in the most fashionable of doublets – by the middle of the 1480s, when the portrait was commissioned, no Bruges merchant wanted to appear too pious. Opposite, the Virgin gets the full stereotypical treatment from the oval face and the almond-shaped eyes through to full cheeks, thin nose and hunched lower lip.

Archeologisch Museum (Archeological Museum)

Mariastraat 36a. Tues–Sun 9.30am–12.30pm & 1.30–5pm; €2. The city's Archeologisch Museum is a particularly modest affair, whose ground-floor displays take a shot at explaining the role of the archeologist in preserving the city's past. The labelling is, however, only in Dutch and the same applies upstairs, where the most substantial section is devoted to the city's medieval tanners, featuring an assortment of decrepit leather shoes recovered from various digs.

St Salvatorskathedraal (Cathedral of the Holy Saviour)

Mon 2–5.30pm, Tues–Fri 9am–noon & 2–5.30pm, Sat 9am–noon & 2–3.30pm, Sun 9–10am & 2–5pm; free. St Salvatorskathedraal is a bulky Gothic edifice that mostly dates from the late thirteenth century, though the Flamboyant Gothic ambulatory was added some two centuries later. A parish church for most of its history, it was only made a cathedral in 1834 following the destruction of St Donatian's (see p.62) by the French. This change of status prompted lots of ecclesiastical rumblings – nearby Onze Lieve Vrouwekerk (see p.68) was bigger and its spire higher – and when part of St Salvators went up in smoke in 1839, the opportunity was taken to make its tower higher and grander in a romantic rendition of the Romanesque style.

▼ ST SALVATORSKATHEDRAAL

Recently cleaned, the cathedral's nave has emerged from centuries of accumulated grime, but remains a cheerless, cavernous affair. The star turn is the set of eight paintings by Jan van Orley displayed in the transepts. Commissioned in the 1730s, the paintings were used for the manufacture of a matching set of tapestries from a Brussels workshop; remarkably enough, these have survived too and hang in sequence in the choir and nave. Each of the eight scenes is a fluent, dramatic composition featuring a familiar episode from the life of Christ – from the Nativity to the Resurrection – complete with a handful of animals, including a remarkably determined Palm Sunday donkey. The tapestries are actually mirror images of the paintings as the weavers worked with the rear of the tapestries uppermost on their looms; the weavers also had sight of the tapestry paintings – or rather cartoon copies, as the originals were too valuable to be kept beside the looms. Also in the choir are the painted escutcheons of the members of the Order of the Golden Fleece, which met here in 1478 (see box below).

Entered from the nave, the cathedral **treasury** (daily except Sat 2–5pm; €2.50) occupies the adjoining neo-Gothic chapter house, whose nine rooms are packed with ecclesiastical tackle, from religious paintings and statues through to an assortment of reliquaries, vestments and croziers. The labelling is poor, however, so it's a good idea to

The Order of the Golden Fleece

Philip the Good, the Duke of Burgundy, invented the Order of the Golden Fleece in 1430 on the occasion of his marriage to Isabella of Portugal. Duke since 1419, Philip had spent much of his time curbing the power of the Flemish cities – including Bruges – but he was too economically dependent on them to feel entirely secure. To bolster his position, the duke was always looking for ways to add lustre to his dynasty, hence his creation of the Order of the Golden Fleece, an exclusive, knightly club that harked back to the (supposed) age of chivalry. The choice of the name was a complimentary nod both to the wool weavers of Flanders, who provided him with most of his money, and to the legends of classical Greece. In the Greek story, a winged ram named Chrysomallus – gifted with the power of speech and a golden fleece – saved the life of Phrixus, presented him with his fleece and then flew off to become the constellation of Aries; it was this same fleece that Jason and the Argonauts later sought to recover. The Order's emblem was a golden ram.

Philip stipulated that membership of the Order be restricted to "noblemen in name and proven in valour … born and raised in legitimate wedlock". He promptly picked the membership and appointed himself Grand Master. It was all something of a con trick, but it went down a treat and the 24 knights who were offered membership duly turned up at the first meeting in Lille in 1431. Thereafter, the Order met fairly regularly, gathering together for some mutual back-slapping, feasting and the exchange of presents. Bruges and Ghent were two favourite venues, and the Order met three times in the former: at St Donatian's Cathedral in 1431, at the Onze Lieve Vrouwekerk in 1468, and at St Salvatorskathedraal in 1478. However, when the Habsburgs swallowed up Burgundy in the late fifteenth century, the Order was rendered obsolete and the title "Grand Master" became just one of the family's many dynastic trinkets.

pick up the English–language mini–guide at the entrance. Room B holds the treasury's finest painting, a gruesome, minutely observed oak-panel triptych, *The Martyrdom of St Hippolytus*, by Dieric Bouts (1410–75) and Hugo van der Goes (d.1482). In Room E, also look out for the coin-like tokens the church wardens once gave to the poor. Each is inscribed with an entitlement – "W.B.", for instance, means bread for a week.

Diamantmuseum Brugge (Bruges Diamond Museum)

Katelijnestraat 43 ☎ 050 34 20 56, ⓦ www.diamondmuseum.be. Daily 10.30am–5.30pm; €6, or €9 with diamond-polishing demonstration. A privately owned museum, the Diamantmuseum Brugge, opposite the east end of Wijngaardstraat, tracks through the history of the city's diamond industry and displays many different sorts of diamond in various settings. There are daily demonstrations of diamond polishing at 12.15pm.

Stoofstraat and Walplein

Strolling south from Sint Janshospitaal along Mariastraat, cross the canal and take the first right turn along L-shaped Stoofstraat, Bruges's narrowest street, whose old terrace houses, now little ateliers and souvenir shops, were once home to the city's prostitutes, who picked up sticks and departed decades ago.

Stoofstraat leads into the Walplein, a pleasant square flanked by the Huisbrouwerij De Halve Maan (Half Moon Brewery; ☎ 050 33 26 97, ⓦ www.halvemaan.be; guided tours: April–Oct daily 11am–4pm, Sat until 5pm; Nov–March Mon–Fri at 11am

▲ HUISBROUWERIJ DE HALVE MAAN

& 3pm, Sat & Sun hourly 11am–4pm; €5), whose forty-minute guided tours include a glass of the brewery's most popular beer, Brugse Zot.

The Begijnhof

Daily 9am–6.30pm or sunset; free. At the south end of Walplein, the antique terrace houses of Wijngaardstraat are crammed with souvenir shops, bars and restaurants. It's all rather depressing, but there's relief near at hand in the much more appealing, if just as over-visited, Begijnhof, where, just over the bridge and through the gate from Wijngaardstraat, a rough circle of old and infinitely pretty whitewashed houses surrounds a central green. The best time to visit is in spring, when a carpet of daffodils pushes up between the wispy elms, creating one of the most photographed scenes in Bruges. There were once begijnhofs all over Belgium, and this is one of the few to have survived in good nick. They date back to the twelfth century, when a Liège priest, a certain Lambert le Bègue, encouraged widows and unmarried women to live in communities, the better to do pious acts, especially caring for the sick. These communities were different from convents in so far as the inhabitants – the beguines (*begijns*) – did not have to take conventual vows and had the right to return to the secular world if they wished. Margaret, Countess of Flanders, founded Bruges's Begijnhof in 1245 and, although most of the houses now standing date from the eighteenth century, the medieval layout has survived intact, preserving the impression of the Begijnhof as a self-contained village, with access controlled through two large gates.

The houses are still in private hands, but, with the beguines long gone, they are now occupied by Benedictine nuns, who you'll see flitting around in their habits. Only one of the houses is open to the public – the Begijnenhuisje (Mon–Sat 10am–noon & 1.45–5pm, Sun 10.45am–noon & 1.45–5pm; €2), a pint-sized celebration of the simple life of the beguines. The prime exhibit here is the *schapraai*, a traditional beguine's cupboard, which was a frugal combination of dining table, cutlery cabinet and larder.

The Minnewater

Just metres from the more southerly of the Begijnhof's two gates is the Minnewater, often hyped as the city's "Lake of Love". The tag certainly gets the canoodlers going, but in fact the lake – more a large pond – started life as a city harbour. The distinctive stone lock house at the head of the Minnewater recalls its earlier function, though it's actually a very fanciful nineteenth-century reconstruction of the medieval original. The Poertoren, on the west bank at the far end of the lake, is more authentic, its brown brickwork dating from 1398 and once part of the city wall. This is where the city kept its gunpowder – hence the name, "powder tower".

Beside the Poertoren, a footbridge spans the southern end of the Minnewater to reach the leafy expanse of Minnewaterpark, which trails north back towards Wijngaardstraat.

▼ THE BEGIJNHOF

Shops

Bilbo

Noordzandstraat 82 ☎ 050 33 40 11, ⓦ www.bilbo.be. Mon–Sat 10am–6.30pm, Sun 2–6pm. The most popular CD shop in town, especially amongst the city's young people, thanks to its bargain-basement prices and large selection of mainstream pop and rock – although there's not much in the way of service or presentation.

The Chocolate Line

Simon Stevinplein 19 ☎ 050 34 10 90, ⓦ www.thechocolateline.be. Mon & Sun 10.30am–6pm, Tues–Sat 9.30am–6pm. Probably the best chocolate shop in town, serving up quality chocolates, handmade on the premises using natural ingredients – so not surprisingly, it's more expensive than most of its many rivals. Chocolate truffles and figurines are a speciality. Boxes of mixed chocolates are sold in various sizes: a 250g box costs €10.

Claeys

Katelijnestraat 54 ☎ 050 33 98 19, ⓦ www.claeysantique.com. Daily 9am–6pm. Diane Claeys studied lace history and design in various museums in Europe before opening this shop in 1980. She now sells handmade, antique-style lace, from handkerchiefs to edging and tablecloths, and also sometimes organizes lace exhibitions here.

Classics

Oude Burg 32 ☎ 050 33 90 58. Tues–Sat 10am–noon & 2–6pm. A mixed bag of an art shop selling everything from fine art, tapestries and antiques to more modern objects in traditional styles, collected from around the world. Also stocks Indian textiles. Affordable prices.

Decorte

Noordzandstraat 23 ☎ 050 33 46 07. Mon–Sat 9am–6pm. Stationery nirvana, with splendid fountain pens, coloured pencils, ink pots, wrapping paper, cards and writing paper, at prices to suit every budget.

Kasimir's Antique Studio

Rozenhoedkaai 3 ☎ 050 34 56 61. Mon–Sat 10.30am–12.30pm & 2–6pm. Antiques don't come cheap in Bruges, and Kasimir's is no exception, but the old furniture on sale here is first-rate, and there's an interesting assortment of old knick-knacks – from ceramics to glassware – too.

Knapp Targa

Zuidzandstraat 18–22 ☎ 050 33 31 27, ⓦ www.knapp-targa.be. Mon–Sat 10am–6.30pm. Arguably the most enjoyable fashion shop in town, Knapp Targa's chic repertoire of top-quality clothes for men and women ranges from the adventurous – or even challenging – to the classic, with labels including Burberry, DKNY, Paul Smith and Coast.

Leonidas

Katelijnestraat 24 ☎ 050 34 69 41. Mon–Sat 9am–7pm, Sun 10am–6pm. Part of the large and popular Belgian chain, this chocolate shop offers a wide selection of pralines and candy confectionery all at very competitive prices (€4.50 for 250g), though their products are more sugary than those of their more exclusive rivals. As with all chocolate shops along Katelijnestraat, expect queues in the summer.

Markets

Bruges has a weekly food and flower market on the Markt (Wed 8am–1pm) and a bigger and better weekly food and general goods market on 't Zand (Sat 8am–1pm). There's also a flea market along the Dijver and on the neighbouring Vismarkt (mid-March to mid-Nov Sat & Sun 10am–6pm), though there are more souvenir and craft stalls here than bric-à-brac places, and the tourist crowds mean that bargains are few and far between. If you're after a bargain, you might consider popping over to the much larger flea markets in Ghent (see p.125).

Louis Delhaize

Oude Burg 22. Mon–Sat 8.30am–6.30pm. Supermarkets are very thin on the ground in central Bruges, but this fills the gap, selling all the basics including fresh fruit, bread, beer and cheese.

De Meester

Dijver 2 ☎050 33 29 52. Mon–Sat 8.30am–noon & 1.30–6.30pm. De Meester (aka De Brugse Boekhandel) is good for books about Bruges, both past and present, and sells a wide range of city maps. It's also reasonably strong on several other topics, notably historical subjects, literature from home and abroad, cookery and gardening.

Neuhaus

Steenstraat 66 ☎050 33 15 30, ⊛www.neuhaus.be. Mon–Sat 10am–6pm, Sun 1.30–6pm. Belgium's best chocolate chain sells superb and beautifully presented chocolates. Check out their specialities such as the handmade Caprices – pralines stuffed with crispy nougat, fresh cream and soft-centred chocolate – and the delicious Manons – stuffed white chocolates, which come with fresh cream, vanilla and coffee fillings. €11 for a 250g box.

Pollentier

St-Salvatorskerkhof 8 ☎050 33 18 04. Tues–Fri 2–6pm, Sat 10am–noon & 2–6pm. This antiquarian hideaway specializes in old and contemporary prints, and also offers a framing service. Seascapes, hunting scenes and Bruges cityscapes predominate, but there are many other subjects as well.

Quicke

Zuidzandstraat 23 ☎050 33 23 00, ⊛www.quicke.be. Mon & Sat 10am–6.30pm, Tues–Thurs 9.30am–6.30pm. The top shoe shop in Bruges, Quicke showcases the great European seasonal collections, featuring exclusive designers such as Prada and Miu Miu. Expensive, naturally.

Standaard Boekhandel

Steenstraat 88 ☎050 34 26 70. Mon–Sat 8.30am–6pm, Sun 2–6pm. Proficient and efficient chain bookshop, with a small English-language fiction section downstairs and a comprehensive range of travel guides, city maps and hiking maps up above.

De Striep

Katelijnestraat 42 ☎050 33 71 12. Mon 1.30–7pm, Tues–Sat 9am–12.30pm & 1.30–7pm, Sun 2–6pm. The only comic-strip specialist in town, stocking everything from run-of-the-mill cheapies to collector's items in Dutch, French and even English.

Cafés

De Bron
Katelijnestraat 82 ☎ 050 33 45 26.
Tues–Sat 11.45am–2pm. Many of
the city's cafés and restaurants
offer vegetarian dishes, but this
pleasant little place is the only
exclusively vegetarian spot per
se, offering fresh, organic food,
with mains from €10.

Detavernier, Tearoom Carpe Diem
Wijngaardstraat 8. Mon–Sat 9am–6pm.
Wijngaardstraat may heave
with tourists and have some
pretty average restaurants, but
this pleasant little tea room,
attached to a bakery-patisserie,
serves delicious light meals and
cakes. One room is kitted out
in antique style, with oodles
of wood panelling, a second
is more modern, and there's a
mini terrace at the back.

't Eekhoetje
Eekhoutstraat 3. Daily except
Wed 8am–6.30pm. Bright
and airy tearoom, with a
small courtyard, just a short
walk from the crowds of
Huidenvettersplein. The
efficient and friendly staff
serve a good selection of tasty

snacks and light meals such as
omelettes, pasta and toasties;
there's also a licensed bar and
a sandwich deli offering cold
fillings and hot pasties.

Gran Kaffee de Passage
Dweersstraat 26. Daily 6pm–midnight,
kitchen till 10.30pm. This lively
café is extremely popular with
backpackers, many of whom have
bunked down in the adjacent
Passage Hostel (see p.146). There's
a good and filling line in Flemish
food, with many dishes cooked
in beer, as well as mussels and
vegetarian options. Not much in
the way of frills, but then main
courses only cost €10–14.

Laurent
Steenstraat 79c. Daily 9am–5.30pm.
Cheap and cheerful café metres
from the cathedral. No points
for décor or atmosphere, but
the snacks are filling and fresh
and the pancakes first-rate. Very
popular with locals.

Lokkedize
Korte Vulderstraat 33. Wed–Sun
6pm–midnight Attracting a
youthful crowd, this sympathetic
café-bar – all subdued lighting,
fresh flowers and jazz music
– serves up a good line in
Mediterranean (especially

▲ LOKKEDIZE

Greek) food, with main courses averaging around €11 and bar snacks from €7.

De Verbeelding

Oude Burg 26. Tues–Sat 11.30am–11.30pm. Low-key, amenable café-bar serving a reasonably satisfying range of salads, pastas and tapas. Few would say the food was brilliant, but it is inexpensive and – at its best – very tasty. Main courses around €10, half that for tapas. Handy for the Markt.

Restaurants

Cafedraal

Zilverstraat 38 ☎ 050 34 08 45, ⓦ www.cafedraal.be. Mon–Sat noon–3pm & 6–11pm. Fashionable and justifiably popular restaurant decked out in ersatz medieval style, with oodles of wood panelling, a big open fire in winter and an outside garden terrace in summer. The menu runs the gamut of French and Flemish dishes, but it's hard to beat the North Sea bouillabaisse or the lobster and veal cooked in mustard. Main courses around €20–25.

Christophe

Garenmarkt 34 ☎ 050 34 48 92. Mon & Thurs–Sun 7pm–1am. Convivial, pocket–sized restaurant with attractive, informal decor and a small but choice menu of French and Flemish dishes. Daily specials are a feature and prices are very reasonable, with main courses averaging around €20.

Den Dyver

Dijver 5 ☎ 050 33 60 69. Mon, Tues & Fri–Sun noon–2pm & 6.30–9pm, Wed & Thurs 6.30–9pm. Top-flight restaurant specializing in traditional Flemish dishes cooked in beer – the quail and rabbit are magnificent, though the seafood runs them close. The decor is plush and antique, with tapestries on the wall beneath an ancient wood-beam ceiling. The service is attentive, but not unduly so, and the only real negative is the Muzak, which can be tiresome. Popular with an older clientele. Reservations advised. Mains around €25.

L'Intermède

Wulfhagestraat 3 ☎ 050 33 16 74. Tues–Sat noon–1.30pm & 7–9.30pm. Tastefully decorated and very chic little restaurant serving

▲ DEN DYVER

exquisite French cuisine with a Flemish twist. Prices are reasonable and it's away from the tourist zone – which is very much to its advantage. Mains €18–24.

Patrick Devos "De Zilveren Pauw"

Zilverstraat 41 ☎050 33 55 66, ⓦwww.patrickdevos.be. Mon–Fri noon–1.30pm & 7–9pm, Sat 7–9pm. One of Bruges' premier restaurants, presided over by Patrick Devos, a great name in Belgian cooking and the designer of such treats as jelly of seafood perfumed with garlic, and duck with rhubarb. Starters begin at around €30, main courses €35, the set menus much more. It's a formal – some would say staid – establishment, and reservations are essential.

Tanuki

Oude Gentweg 1 ☎050 34 75 12. Wed–Sun noon–2pm & 6.30–9.30pm; closed two weeks in Jan & July. The best Japanese restaurant in town and perhaps, if you've been here a long time, a welcome break from the heavy sauces of Belgian cuisine. The menu features all the usual Japanese favourites – noodles, sushi and sashimi – and prices are very competitive, with most dishes around €12.50.

De Visscherie

Vismarkt 8 ☎050 33 02 12, ⓦwww .visscherie.be. Daily except Tues noon–2pm & 7–10pm. Arguably the city's premier seafood restaurant, *De Visscherie* manages to be smart and relaxed at the same time. A well-presented and imaginative menu features such delights as a spectacularly tasty fish soup (€14) and cod cooked in traditional Flemish style (€32). The restaurant

▲ DE VISSCHERIE

occupies a spacious nineteenth-century mansion a short walk south of the Burg, but the decor has some intriguing modern touches – small sculptures and so on – and the chairs are supremely comfortable.

Bars and clubs

B-in

Mariastraat 38 ☎050 31 13 00, ⓦwww.b-in.be. Tues–Sat 10am–3am, Fri & Sat until 5am. Free entry. The coolest place in town, this slick bar-cum-club is kitted out in attractive modern style with low seats and an eye-grabbing mix of coloured fluorescent tubes

▼ B-IN

▲ L'ESTAMINET

and soft ceiling lights. Guest
DJs play funky, uplifting house
and the drinks and cocktails
are reasonably priced. Attracts
a relaxed and friendly crowd,
and gets going about 11pm. It's
located at the far end of the
Oud St-Jan exhibition-cum-
shopping centre off Mariastraat.

De Bolero
Garenmarkt 32. Mon, Tues &
Thurs–Sun from 9pm. Currently the
only gay and lesbian bar/club
in town, hosting regular dance
evenings with a wide range of
sounds, from Abba to house.
Entrance is free and the drinks
aren't too over-priced.

Het Brugs Beertje
Kemelstraat 5. Daily except Tues & Wed
4pm–1am. This small and friendly
speciality beer bar claims a stock
of three hundred beers, which
aficionados reckon is one of
the best selections in Belgium.
There are tasty snacks too,
including cheeses and salad, but
note that the place is very much
on the (backpacker) tourist trail.

L'Estaminet
Park 5. Daily except Mon
11.30am–1am or later, Thurs from
4pm. Groovy café-bar with a
relaxed neighbourhood feel
and (for Bruges) a diverse and

cosmopolitan clientele. Rickety
furniture both inside and on the
large outside terrace adds to the
flavour of the place, as does the
world music backtrack, while
the first-rate beer menu skilfully
picks its way through Belgium's
myriad beers.

Ma Rica Rokk
't Zand 7 ☎050 33 83 58, ⊛www
.maricarokk.com. Daily from 10am
till late. Atmospheric spot with
sparse functional decor that has
long been a local favourite with
students and townies alike. There's
a youthful clientele, zippy service,
a competent beer menu, a
summer terrace and, at weekends,
some of the best music in town,
with house especially popular.
Serves Illy coffee too.

Wijnbar Est
Noordzandstraat 34 ☎050 33 38 39.
Mon, Thurs & Sun 5pm–midnight,
Fri 5pm–1am & Sat 3pm–1am. The
best wine bar in town, with a
friendly and relaxed atmosphere,
an extensive cellar and over 25
different wines available by the
glass every day – it's especially
strong on New World vintages,
and also serves a selection of
cheeses in the evening. There's
live (and free) jazz, blues and
folk music every Sunday from
8pm to 10.30pm.

The Groeninge Museum

The Groeninge Museum (Dijver 12; Tues–Sun 9.30am–5pm; €8, including Arentshuis Museum, see p.66) possesses one of the world's finest samples of early Flemish paintings, from Jan van Eyck through to Hieronymus Bosch and Jan Provoost. These paintings make up the kernel of the museum's permanent collection, but there are later (albeit lesser) pieces on display too, reaching into the twentieth century, with paintings by the likes of Constant Permeke and Paul Delvaux.

The Groeninge has just eleven rooms, chronologically arranged; the early Flemish paintings are concentrated in Rooms 1 to 4, Rooms 5 and 6 are usually devoted to the seventeenth and eighteenth centuries, and Rooms 7 to 11 continue on into 1900s. The description below details some of the most important works and, although the works in the collection are regularly rotated, you can expect most if not all the ones described to be on display.

Jan van Eyck

Arguably the greatest of the early Flemish masters, Jan van Eyck (1385–1441) lived and worked in Bruges from 1430 until his death eleven years later. He was a key figure in the development of oil painting, modulating its tones to create paintings of extraordinary clarity and realism. The Groeninge has two gorgeous examples of his work in its permanent collection, beginning with the miniature portrait of his wife, Margareta van Eyck, painted in 1439 and bearing his motto, "als ich can" (the best I can do).

The painting is very much a private picture and one that had no commercial value, marking a small step away from the sponsored art – and religious preoccupations – of previous Flemish artists.

The second Eyck painting is the remarkable *Madonna and Child with Canon George van der Paele*, a glowing and richly symbolic work with three figures surrounding the Madonna; the kneeling canon, St George (his patron saint)

▼ MARGARETA VAN EYCK, JAN VAN EYCK

Jan van Eyck's most magnificent painting, the extraordinary *Adoration of the Mystic Lamb*, is displayed in St Baafskathedraal in Ghent (see p.111).

and St Donatian, to whom he is being presented. St George doffs his helmet to salute the infant Christ and speaks by means of the Hebrew word "Adonai" (Lord) inscribed on his chin strap, while Jesus replies through the green parrot in his left hand: folklore asserted that this type of parrot was fond of saying "Ave", the Latin for welcome. The canon's face is exquisitely executed, down to the sagging jowls and the bulging blood vessels at his temple, while the glasses and book in his hand add to his air of deep contemplation. Audaciously, Van Eyck has broken with tradition by painting the canon amongst the saints rather than as a lesser figure – a distinct nod to the humanism that was gathering pace in contemporary Bruges. The painting also celebrates the wealth of Bruges in the luxurious clothes and furnishings: the floor tiles are of Spanish design, the geometric

tapestry at the feet of the Madonna comes from Asia and St Donatian is decked out in jewel-encrusted vestments.

Rogier van der Weyden

The Groeninge possesses two fine and roughly contemporaneous copies of paintings by Rogier van der Weyden (1399–1464), onetime official city painter to Brussels. The first is the tiny *Portrait of Philip the Good*, in which the pallor of the duke's aquiline features, along with the brightness of his hatpin and chain of office, are skilfully balanced by the sombre cloak and hat. The second and much larger painting, *St Luke painting the Portrait of Our Lady*, is a rendering of a popular if highly improbable legend which claimed that Luke painted Mary – thereby becoming the patron saint of painters. The painting is notable for the detail of its Flemish background and the cheeky-chappie smile of the baby Christ.

Hugo van der Goes

One of the most gifted of the early Flemish artists, Hugo van der Goes (d.1482) is a shadowy figure, though it is known that he became master of the painters' guild in Ghent in 1467. Eight years later, he entered a Ghent priory as a lay-brother, perhaps related to the prolonged bouts of acute depression which afflicted him. Few of his paintings have survived, but these exhibit a superb compositional balance and a keen observational eye. His last work, the luminescent *Death of Our Lady*, is here at the Groeninge, though it was originally hung in the abbey at Koksijde on the coast.

▲ DEATH OF OUR LADY, VAN DER GOES

PLACES

Bruges: The Groeninge Museum

▲ TRIPTYCH OF WILLEM MOREEL, MEMLING

Sticking to religious legend, the Apostles have been miraculously transported to Mary's deathbed, where, in a state of agitation, they surround the prostrate woman. Mary is dressed in blue, but there are no signs of luxury, reflecting both der Goes' asceticism and his polemic – the artist may well have been appalled by the church's love of glitter and gold.

The Master of the St Ursula Legend

Another highlight of the Groeninge are the two matching panels of *The Legend of St Ursula*, the work of an unknown fifteenth-century artist known as the Master of the St Ursula Legend. The panels, each of which displays five miniature scenes, were probably inspired by the twelfth-century discovery of the supposed bones of St Ursula and the women who were massacred with her in Cologne seven centuries before – a sensational find that would certainly have been common knowledge in Bruges. Surfacing in the ninth century, the original legend describes St Ursula as a British princess who avoids an unwanted marriage by going on a pilgrimage to Rome accompanied by ten female companions, sometimes referred to as nuns or virgins. On their

way back, a tempest blows their ship off course and they land at Cologne where the (pagan) Huns promptly slaughter them. Pious women who suffered for the faith always went down a storm in medieval Christendom, but somewhere along the line the ten women became ten thousand – possibly because the buckets of bones found in Cologne were from an old public burial ground and had nothing to do with Ursula and her chums.

Hans Memling

The work of Hans Memling (1430–94) is represented by a pair of Annunciation panels from a triptych – gentle, romantic representations of an angel and Mary in contrasting shades of grey, a monochrome technique known as grisaille. Here also is Memling's *Moreel Triptych*, in which the formality of the design is offset by the warm colours and the gentleness of the detail – St Giles strokes the fawn and the knight's hand lies on the donor's shoulder. The central panel depicts saints Giles and Maurus to either side of St Christopher with a backdrop of mountains, clouds and sea. St Christopher, the patron saint of travellers, carries Jesus on his shoulders in an abbreviated reference to the original story which has the saint, who made his living lugging travellers across a river, carrying a child who becomes impossibly heavy. In the way of such things, it turns out that the child is Jesus and the realization turns Christopher, Christian. The side panels show the donors and their sixteen children along with their patron saints – the knight St William for Willem Moreel, a wealthy spice trader and financier, and St Barbara for his wife. There are more Memling paintings at St Janshospitaal, see p.70.

Gerard David and Hieronymus Bosch

Born near Gouda, the Dutchman Gerard David (c.1460–1523) moved to Bruges in his early twenties. Soon admitted into the local painters' guild, he quickly rose through the ranks, becoming the city's leading artistic light after the death of Memling. Official commissions rained in on David, mostly for religious paintings, which he approached in a formal manner but with a fine eye for detail. The Groeninge holds two excellent examples

of his work, starting with the *Baptism of Christ* triptych, in which a boyish, lightly bearded Christ is depicted as part of the Holy Trinity in the central panel. There's also one of David's few secular ventures in the Groeninge, the intriguing *Judgement of Cambyses*, painted on two oak panels. Based on a Persian legend related by Herodotus, the first panel's background shows the corrupt judge Sisamnes accepting a bribe, with his subsequent arrest by grim-faced aldermen filling the foreground. The aldermen crowd in on Sisamnes with a palpable sense of menace and, as the king sentences him to be flayed alive, a sweaty look of fear sweeps over the judge's face. In the gruesome second panel the king's servants carry out the judgement, applying themselves to the task with clinical detachment. Behind, in the top-right corner, the fable is completed with the judge's son dispensing justice from his father's old chair, which is now draped with the flayed skin. Completed in 1498, the painting was hung in the council chamber by the city burghers to encourage honesty amongst its magistrates and as a sort of public apology for the imprisonment of Archduke Maximilian in Bruges in 1488. Maximilian would almost certainly have appreciated the painting – even if the gesture was itself too little, too late – as the king dispenses his judgement without reference to either the Church or God, a subtext of secular authority very much to his tastes.

The Groeninge also holds Hieronymus Bosch's (1450–1516) *Last Judgement*, a trio of oak panels crammed

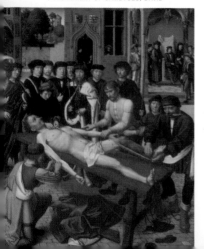

▼ JADGEMENT OF CAMBYSES, DAVID

▲ LAST JUDGEMENT, BOSCH

with mysterious beasts, microscopic mutants and scenes of awful cruelty – men boiled in a pit or cut in half by a giant knife. It looks like unbridled fantasy, but in fact the scenes were read as symbols, a sort of strip cartoon of legend, proverb and tradition. Indeed Bosch's religious orthodoxy is confirmed by the appeal his work had for that most Catholic of Spanish kings, Philip II.

Jan Provoost and Adriaen Isenbrant

There's more grim symbolism in the crowded and melodramatic *Last Judgement* by Jan Provoost (1465–1529), painted for the Stadhuis in 1525, and his striking *The Miser and Death*, which portrays the merchant with his money in one panel, trying desperately to pass a promissory note to the grinning skeleton in the next. Provoost's career was typical of many of the Flemish artists of the early sixteenth century. Initially he worked in the Flemish manner, his style greatly influenced by

Gerard David, but from about 1521 his work was reinvigorated by contact with the German painter and engraver Albrecht Dürer, who had himself been inspired by the artists of the early Italian Renaissance. Provoost moved around too, working in Valenciennes and Antwerp, before settling in Bruges in 1494. One of his Bruges contemporaries was Adriaen Isenbrant (d.1551), whose speciality was small, precisely executed panels. His *Virgin and Child* triptych is a good example of his technically proficient work.

Bernard van Orley

Bernard van Orley (1488–1541) was a long-time favourite of the Habsburg officials in Brussels until his Protestant sympathies put him in the commercial doghouse. A versatile artist, Orley produced action-packed paintings of Biblical scenes, often backdropped by classical buildings in the Renaissance style, and also designed stained-glass windows and tapestries. He is represented in the Groeninge collection by the strip-cartoon-style *Legend of St Rochus*. A fourteenth-century saint hailing from Montpellier in France, Rochus was in northern Italy on a pilgrimage to Rome when the plague struck. He abandoned his journey to tend to the sick and promptly discovered he had miraculous healing powers. This did not stop him from catching the plague himself, but fortunately a remarkable dog was on hand to nurse him back to health. Recovered, Rochus went back home, but his relatives failed to recognize him and he was imprisoned as an impostor, and died there – a hard luck story if ever there was one.

Pieter Pourbus, Frans the Elder and Frans the Younger

The museum's collection of late sixteenth- and seventeenth-century paintings isn't especially strong, but there's enough to demonstrate the period's watering down of religious themes in favour of more secular preoccupations. Pieter Pourbus (1523–84) is well represented by a series of austere and often surprisingly unflattering portraits of the movers and shakers of his day. There's also his *Last Judgement*, a much larger but atypical work,

crammed with muscular men and fleshy women; completed in 1551, its inspiration came from Michelangelo's Sistine Chapel. Born in Gouda, Pourbus moved to Bruges in his early twenties, becoming the leading local portraitist of his day as well as squeezing in work as a civil engineer and cartographer. Pieter was the first of an artistic dynasty with his son, Frans the Elder (1545–81), jumping municipal ship to move to Antwerp as Bruges slipped into the economic doldrums. Frans was a noted portraitist too, but his success was trifling in comparison with that of his son, Frans the Younger (1569–1622), who became one of Europe's most celebrated portraitists, working for the Habsburgs and the Medicis amongst a bevy of powerful families. In the permanent collection is a fine example of his work, an exquisite double portrait of the Archdukes Albert and Isabella.

Jacob van Oost the Elder

Jacob van Oost the Elder (1603–71) was the city's most prominent artist during the Baroque period and the Groeninge has a substantial sample of his work, though – by comparison with what has gone before – his canvases are pretty meagre stuff (and are often not displayed at all). His *Portrait of a Theologian*, for example, is a stultifyingly formal and didactic affair only

▲ VISITORS AT THE GROENINGE

partly redeemed by its crisp draughtsmanship, while his *Portrait of a Bruges Family* drips with bourgeois sentimentality.

The Symbolists

The Groeninge has a substantial collection of nineteenth- and early twentieth-century Belgian art, but not nearly enough gallery space to display it all – and consequently even the more significant paintings aren't always on display. Nonetheless, obvious highlights include the paintings of the Symbolists, amongst whom Fernand Khnopff (1858–1921) is represented by *Secret Reflections*, not one of his better paintings perhaps, but interesting in so far as its lower panel, showing St Janshospitaal (see p.70) reflected in a canal, confirms one of the Symbolists' favourite conceits: "Bruges the dead city". This was inspired by Georges Rodenbach's novel *Bruges la Morte*, a highly stylized musing on love and obsession first published in 1892. The book kickstarted the craze for visiting Bruges, the "dead city", where the action unfolds. The upper panel of Khnopff's painting is a play on appearance and desire, but it's really rather feeble, unlike his later attempts, in which he painted his sister, Marguerite, again and again, using her refined, almost plastic beauty to stir a vague sense of passion – for she's desirable and utterly unobtainable in equal measure.

The Expressionists and Surrealists

The museum has a healthy sample of the work of the talented Constant Permeke (1886–1952). Wounded in World War I, Permeke's grim wartime experiences helped

him develop a distinctive Expressionist style in which his subjects – usually agricultural workers, fishermen and so forth – were monumental in form, but invested with sombre, sometimes threatening emotion. His charcoal drawing the *Angelus* is a typically dark and earthy representation of Belgian peasant life dated 1934. In similar vein is the enormous *Last Supper* by Gustave van de Woestijne (1881–1947), another excellent example of Belgian Expressionism, with Jesus and the disciples, all elliptical eyes and restrained movement, trapped within prison-like walls.

Also noteworthy is the spookily stark surrealism of *Serenity* by Paul Delvaux (1897–1994). One of the most interesting of Belgium's modern artists, Delvaux started out as an Expressionist but came to – and stayed with – Surrealism in the 1930s. Two of his pet motifs were train stations, in one guise or another, and nude or semi-nude women set against some sort of classical backdrop. The intention was to usher the viewer into the unconscious with dream-like images where every perspective was exact, and there is indeed something very unsettling about his vision, largely because of the impeccable craftsmanship. At their best, his paintings achieve an almost palpable sense of foreboding – and *Serenity* is a first-class example.

The Groeninge also owns a couple of minor oils and a number of etchings and drawings by James Ensor (1860–1949), one of Belgium's most innovative painters, and Magritte's (1898–1967) characteristically unnerving *The Assault*.

North and east of the Markt

The gentle canals and maze-like cobbled streets of eastern Bruges are extraordinarily pretty, and it's here that the city reveals its depth of character. In this uncrowded part of the centre, which stretches east from Jan van Eyckplein to the old medieval moat, several different types of architecture blend into an almost seamless whole, beginning with the classically picturesque terraces that date from the town's late medieval golden age. The most characteristic architectural feature is the crow-step gable, popular from the fourteenth to the eighteenth century and revived by the restorers of the 1880s and later, but there are also expansive classical mansions and humble cottages. Almost all the buildings are of brick, reflecting the shortage of local stone and the abundance of polder peat, which was used to fire clay bricks, clay being another common commodity hereabouts. Above all, eastern Bruges excels in its detail, surprising the eye again and again with its subtle variety, featuring everything from intimate arched doorways, bendy tiled roofs and wonky chimneys through to a bevy of discreet shrines and miniature statues.

Nevertheless, there are one or two obvious targets for the visitor, beginning with the Kantcentrum (Lace Centre), where you can buy locally made lace, and the city's most unusual church, the adjacent Jeruzalemkerk. In addition, the Folklore Museum holds a passably interesting collection of local bygones, while the Museum Onze-Lieve-Vrouw ter Potterie (Museum of Our Lady of the Pottery) has an intriguing chapel and several fine Flemish tapestries.

St Jakobskerk (Church of St James)

St-Jakobsstraat. April–Sept Mon–Sat 10am–noon & 2–5pm, Sun 2–5pm; free. From the Markt, it's a short stroll north to St Jakobskerk, whose sombre exterior, mostly dating from the fifteenth century, clusters round a chunky tower. In medieval times the church was popular with the foreign merchants who had congregated in Bruges, acting as a sort of prototype community centre; it also marked the western limit of the foreign merchants' quarter. Inside, the church is mainly Baroque, its airy nave interrupted and darkened by a grim marble rood screen with an equally cumbersome high altar lurking beyond. Much more appealing is the handsome early Renaissance burial chapel of Ferry de Gros (d. 1547), to the right of the choir, which sports the elaborate, painted tomb of this well-to-do landowner. Unusually, the tomb has two shelves – on the top are the finely carved effigies of Ferry and his first wife, while below, on the lower shelf, is his second. Here also, above the altar, is an enamelled terracotta medallion of the Virgin and Child imported from Florence some time in the fifteenth century. No one knows quite how it ended up here, but there's no doubt that it influenced Flemish artists of the period – in the same way as Michelangelo's statue in the Onze Lieve Vrouwekerk. The walls of St Jakobskerk are covered with around eighty paintings bequeathed by the city's merchants. They're not an especially distinguished bunch, but look out for the finely executed *Legend of St Lucy*, a panel triptych by the Master of the St Lucy Legend that tracks through the sufferings of this fourth-century saint in some detail; it's located in St Anthony's Chapel – the first chapel on the left-hand side of the nave. In the next chapel along, look out also for the meditative *Madonna and the Seven Sorrows*, a triptych by Pieter Pourbus (1523–84), the leading local artist of his day.

Kraanplein

East of St Jakobskerk lies Kraanplein – Crane Square – whose name recalls one of the medieval city's main attractions, the enormous wooden crane that once unloaded heavy goods from the adjoining river. Before it was covered over, the River Reie ran south from Jan van Eyckplein to the Markt, and the Kraanplein dock was one of the busiest parts of this central waterway. Mounted on a revolving post in the manner of a windmill, the crane's pulleys were worked by means of two large treadmills operated by children – a grim existence by any measure. Installed in 1290 – and only dismantled in 1767 – the crane impressed visitors greatly and was as sure a sign of Bruges's economic success as the Belfort. The crane crops up in the background of several medieval paintings, notably behind St John in Memling's *Mystical Marriage of St Catherine* (see p.72).

Jan van Eyckplein

Just to the north of Kraanplein lies Jan van Eyckplein, one of

▼ JAN VAN EYCKPLEIN

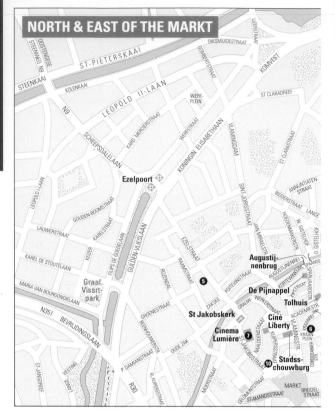

NORTH & EAST OF THE MARKT

the prettiest squares in Bruges, its cobbles backdropped by the easy sweep of the Spiegelrei canal. The centrepiece of the square is an earnest statue of Van Eyck, erected in 1878, whilst on the north side is the Tolhuis, whose fancy Renaissance entrance is decorated with the coat of arms of the dukes of Luxembourg, who long levied tolls here. The Tolhuis dates from the late fifteenth century, but was extensively remodelled in medieval style in the 1870s, as was the Poortersloge (Merchants' Lodge), whose slender tower pokes up above the rooftops on the west side of the square.

Theoretically, any city merchant was entitled to be a member of the Poortersloge, but in fact membership was restricted to the richest and the most powerful. An informal alternative to the Town Hall, it was here that key political and economic decisions were taken and it was also where local bigwigs could drink and gamble discreetly.

The Spiegelrei canal and the Augustijnenbrug

Running east from Jan van Eyckplein, the Spiegelrei canal was once the heart of the foreign merchants' quarter, its frenetic quays overlooked by

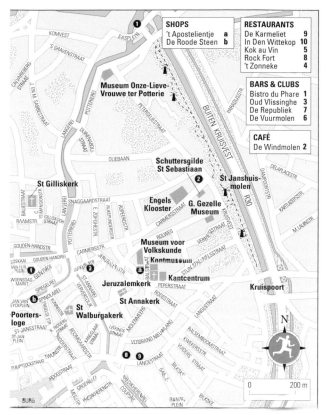

SHOPS	
't Apostelientje	a
De Roode Steen	b

RESTAURANTS	
De Karmeliet	9
In Den Wittekop	10
Kok au Vin	5
Rock Fort	8
't Zonneke	4

BARS & CLUBS	
Bistro du Phare	1
Oud Vlissinghe	3
De Republiek	7
De Vuurmolen	6

CAFÉ	
De Windmolen	2

the trade missions of many of the city's trading partners. The medieval buildings were demolished long ago but have been replaced by an exquisite medley of architectural styles from expansive Classical mansions to pirouetting crow-step gables.

At the far end of Spiegelrei, turn left onto Gouden-Handrei, which, along with adjoining Spaanse Loskaai, flanks an especially attractive sliver of canal that was once used as a quay by Bruges's Spanish merchants. On the far side of the canal stand a string of delightful summer outhouses,

▲ SPIEGELREI CANAL

privately owned and sometimes surprisingly lavish extensions to the demure houses fronting onto Gouden-Handstraat.

At the west end of Spaanse Loskaai is the Augustijnenbrug, the city's oldest surviving bridge, a sturdy three-arched structure dating from 1391. The bridge was built to help the monks of a nearby (and long-demolished) Augustinian monastery get into the city centre speedily; the benches set into the parapet were cut to allow itinerant tradesmen to display their goods here.

Heading south from the bridge is Spanjaardstraat, which was also part of the Spanish enclave. It was here, at no.9, in a house formerly known as De Pijnappel (The Fir Cone), that the founder of the Jesuits, Ignatius Loyola (1491–1556), spent his holidays while he was a student in Paris. He befriended Juan Luis Vives (see p.67), who lodged down the street, but unfortunately his friend's liberality failed to temper Loyola's nascent fanaticism. Spanjaardstraat leads back to Jan van Eyckplein.

St Gilliskerk

St Gilliskerkhof. April–Sept Mon–Sat 10am–noon & 2–5pm, Sun 2–5pm; free. The sturdy brick pile of St Gilliskerk dates from the late thirteenth century, though it was considerably enlarged in the 1460s; the church has a wide and appealing three-aisled nave, but its most distinctive feature is its unusual barrel-vaulted roof, which was added in the eighteenth century. Among the paintings on display, the pick is the Hemelsdale polyptych by the prolific Pieter Pourbus (on the wall just to the right of the main doors). It's a dainty piece of work with the donors at either end sandwiching four scenes from the life of Christ – the Adoration of the Shepherds, the arrival of the Magi, the Flight into Egypt and Jesus' Circumcision. The church also possesses six eighteenth-century paintings illustrating the efforts of the Trinitarian monks to ransom Christian prisoners from the Turks. In themselves, the paintings are distinctly second-rate, but the two near the organ in the top right-hand corner of the church are interesting in their sinister representation of the east – all glowering clouds and gloomy city walls. The other four paintings, in the bottom left-hand corner of the nave, explain the papal foundation, in 1198, of the Trinitarians, an order specifically devoted to the ransom of Christians held by Muslims, and one which enjoyed strong support from St Gilliskerk.

St Walburgakerk

Koningstraat. April–Sept Mon–Sat 10am–noon & 2–5pm, Sun

▲ ST WALBURGAKERK

2–5pm; free.
Southeast of Jan van Eyckplein, St Walburgakerk is a fluent Baroque extravagance built for the Jesuits in the first half of the seventeenth century. Framed by slender pilasters, the sinuous, flowing facade is matched

▲ KANTCENTRUM

by the extravagance of the booming interior, awash with acres of creamy-white paint. The grandiose pulpit, complete with its huffing and puffing cherubs, was the work of Artus II Quellin (1625–1700), an Antwerp woodcarver and sculptor whose family ran a profitable sideline in Baroque pulpits.

The pick of the church's scattering of paintings is a Pieter Claeissens triptych – on the right-hand side of the nave. The central panel depicts a popular legend relating to Philip the Good, a fifteenth-century count of Flanders and the founder of the Order of the Golden Fleece (see p.74). The story goes that as Philip was preparing to fight the French, he encountered the Virgin Mary in a scorched tree; not one to look a gift horse in the mouth, Philip fell to his knees and asked for victory, and his prayers were promptly answered.

St Annakerk

April–Sept Mon–Sat 10am–noon & 2–5pm, Sun 2–5pm; free. Founded in the 1490s, St Annakerk came a cropper in the religious wars of the sixteenth century when the Protestants burnt the place to the ground. Rebuilt in the 1620s, the church is a dinky little structure surmounted by the slenderest of brick towers and set within a pleasant little square. Almost untouched since its reconstruction, the interior is a notably homogeneous example of the Baroque, its barrel-vaulted, single-aisled nave almost drowning in ornately carved, dark-stained wooden panelling. Pride of artistic place going to the marble and porphyry rood screen of 1628, but you can't miss the huge painting of the Last Judgement, completed by Hendrik Herregouts (1633–1724), who painted religious scenes in a score of churches across Dutch-speaking Belgium.

Kantcentrum (Lace Centre)

Peperstraat 3. Mon–Fri 10am–noon & 2–6pm, Sat 10am–noon & 2–5pm; €2.50. Just beyond St Annakerk, at the east end of the Spiegelrei canal, is an old working-class district of low brick cottages, in the middle of which, at the foot of Balstraat, lies a complex of buildings which originally belonged to the wealthy Adornes family, who migrated here from Genoa in the thirteenth century. Inside the complex, the Kantcentrum, on the right-hand side of the entrance, has a couple of busy workshops and offers very informal demonstrations of traditional lace-making in the afternoon (no set times). They sell the stuff, too – both here and in the shop at the ticket kiosk – but it isn't cheap: a smallish Bruges table mat, with two swans, for example, costs €20–25; if you fancy having a go yourself, the shop has all the gubbins.

Jeruzalemkerk (Jerusalem Church)

Same times and ticket as Kantcentrum (see p.95). Across the passageway from the Kantcentrum kiosk is one of the city's real oddities, the Jeruzalemkerk. This was built by the Adornes family in the fifteenth century as an approximate copy of the Church of the Holy Sepulchre in Jerusalem after one of their number, Pieter, had returned from a pilgrimage to the Holy Land. The interior is on two levels: the lower one is dominated by a large and ghoulish altarpiece, decorated with skulls and ladders, in front of which is the black marble tomb of Anselm Adornes, the son of the church's founder, and his wife Margaretha. The pilgrimage

▼ JERUZALEMKERK

didn't bring Anselm much luck – he was murdered in gruesome circumstances in Scotland in 1483 while serving as Bruges's consul. There's more grisliness at the back of the church, where the small vaulted chapel holds a replica of Christ's tomb – you can glimpse the imitation body down the tunnel behind the iron grating. To either side of the main altar, steps ascend to the choir, which is situated right below the eccentric, onion-domed lantern tower.

Kantmuseum (Lace Museum)

Same times and ticket as Kantcentrum. Behind the Jeruzalemkerk, the tiny Kantmuseum is of passing interest for its samples of antique lace. The museum holds fifty-odd examples of old, handmade lace, the most elaborate of which is its sample of late nineteenth-century Chantilly lace. Incidentally, most lace shops in Bruges – and there are lots – sell lace manufactured in the Far East, especially China. The best lace shop in town – for locally made lace – is 't Apostelientje (see p.101), very close to the Kantcentrum at Balstraat 11.

Museum voor Volkskunde (Folklore Museum)

Balstraat 43. Tues–Sun 9.30am–5pm; €3. At the north end of Balstraat, the Museum voor Volkskunde occupies a long line of low-ceilinged almshouses set beside a trim courtyard. The interior holds a varied collection, with the emphasis on the nineteenth and early twentieth centuries, but the labelling is patchy so it's best to pick up an English guidebook at reception. Rooms 1–5 are to the right of the entrance, rooms 6–14 are dead

▲ FOLKLORE MUSEUM

modest but enjoyable display of local costumes and textiles, including several samplers made by trainee lacemakers, and Room 7 is a re-created classroom from circa 1920. Room 11 focuses on popular religion, with an interesting collection of pilgrimage banners plus the wax, silver and iron ex votos that still hang in many Flemish churches. Traditionally, the believer makes a promise to God – say, to behave better – and then asks for a blessing, like the curing of a bad leg. Sometimes the ex voto is hung up once the promise is made, but mostly it's done afterwards, in gratitude for the cure or blessing.

Rooms 13 and 14 hold a display on pipes and tobacco. There are all sorts of antique smokers' paraphernalia – tobacco cutters, lighters, tinder boxes and so forth – but it's the selection of pipes which catches the eye, especially the long, thin ones made of clay. Clay pipes were notoriously brittle, so smokers invested in pipe cases, of which several are exhibited.

ahead. Beside the entrance, in Room 15, De Zwarte Kat – the Black Cat – is a small tavern done out in traditional style and serving ales and snacks.

The string of period shops and workshops includes a confectioner's shop, in Room 2, where in summer there are occasional demonstrations of traditional sweet-making. Next door, in Room 3, is an intriguing assortment of biscuit and chocolate moulds as well as cake decorations (patacons). Made of clay, these patacons were painted by hand in true folksy style, with the three most popular motifs being animals, military scenes and Bible stories. Moving on, Room 6 holds a

The Guido Gezelle Museum

Rolweg 64. Tues–Sun 9.30am–12pm & 1.30–4.30pm; €2. The Guido Gezelle Museum commemorates

Bruges lace

Renowned for the fineness of its thread and beautiful motifs, **Belgian lace** – or Flanders lace as it was formerly known – was once famous the world over. It was worn in the courts of Brussels, Paris, Madrid and London – Queen Elizabeth I of England is said to have had no fewer than three thousand lace dresses – and Bruges was a centre of its production. Handmade lace reached the peak of its popularity in the early nineteenth century, when hundreds of Bruges women worked as home-based lacemakers. The industry was, however, transformed by the arrival of machine-made lace in the 1840s and, by the end of the century, handmade lace had been largely supplanted and most of the remaining lacemakers had gone to work in factories. This highly mechanized industry collapsed after World War I when lace, a symbol of an old and discredited order, suddenly had no place in the wardrobe of most women.

▲ GUIDO GEZELLE MUSEUM

the poet-priest Guido Gezelle (1830–99), a leading figure in nineteenth-century Bruges. Gezelle was born in this substantial brick cottage, which now contains a few personal knick-knacks such as Gezelle's old chair and pipes, plus his death mask, though it's mostly devoted to a biographical account of his life. The labelling is, however, only in Dutch and you really need to be a Gezelle enthusiast to get much out of it. Neither is Gezelle to everyone's tastes. His poetry is pretty average and the fact that he translated Longfellow's *Song of Hiawatha* into Dutch is the sort of detail that bores rather than inspires.

More importantly, Gezelle played a key role in the preservation of many of the city's medieval buildings and was instrumental in the creation of the Gruuthuse Museum. Gezelle believed that the survival of the medieval city symbolized the continuity of the Catholic faith, a mindset similar to that of the city's Flemish nationalists, who resisted change and championed medieval – or at least neo-Gothic – architecture to maintain Flemish "purity". Gezelle resisted cultural change, too: a secular theatre appalled him, prompting him to write: "We are smothered by displays of adultery and incest… and the foundations of the family and of marriage are [being] undermined".

St Janshuismolen and the Kruispoort

At the east end of Rolweg, a long and wide earthen bank marks the path of the old town walls. Perched on top are a quartet of windmills – two clearly visible close by and another two beyond eyeshot, about 300m and 500m to the north. You'd have to be something of a windmill fanatic to want to visit them all, but the nearest two are mildly diverting – and the closest, St Janshuismolen, is in working order, and the only one which is open (April–Sept Sat & Sun 9.30am–12.30pm & 1.30–5pm; €2). South of St Janshuismolen is the Kruispoort, a much-modified

▲ ST JANSHUISMOLEN WINDMILL

Bruges's medieval gates

Of the city's seven medieval gates, four have survived in relatively good condition, though all have been heavily restored. Apart from the Kruispoort (see opposite), these are the Gentpoort, on the southeast edge of the centre on Gentpoortstraat; the Smedenpoort, on the west side of the city centre at the end of Smedenstraat; and the Ezelpoort – Donkey Gate – to the northwest of the centre. All four date from the early fifteenth century and consist of twin, heavily fortified, stone walls and turrets.

and strongly fortified city gate dating from 1402.

Schuttersgilde St Sebastiaan

Carmersstraat 174. May–Sept Tues–Thurs 10am–noon, Sat 2–5pm; Oct–April Tues–Thurs & Sat 2–5pm; €3. At the east end of Carmersstraat, one street up from Rolweg, the guild house of the Schuttersgilde St Sebastiaan – The Marksmen's (or Archers') Guild of St Sebastian – is a large brick pile with a distinctive tower that dates from the middle of the sixteenth century. The city's archers had ceased to be of any military importance by the time of its construction, but the guild had, by then, redefined itself as an exclusive social club where the bigwigs of the day could spend their time hobnobbing. Nowadays, it's still in use as a social-cum-sports club with the archers opting either to shoot at the familiar circular targets or to plonk a replica bird on top of a pole and shoot at it from below – the traditional favourite. All in all, the house is hardly riveting, but it does possess an attractive old dining hall, where a bust of Charles II surmounts the fireplace, recalling the days when the exiled king was a guild member (see box, p.100). Visitors can also drop by the shooting gallery, whose medievalist stained-glass

windows date from the 1950s, and catch a glimpse of the modern clubhouse.

The Engels Klooster (English Convent)

Carmersstraat 85. Mon–Sat 2–4pm & 4.30–5.30pm; free. During his stay in Bruges, the exiled king Charles II worshipped at the Engels Klooster on Carmersstraat. Founded in 1629, the convent was long a haven for English Catholic exiles, though this didn't stop Queen Victoria from popping in during her visit to Belgium in 1843. Nowadays, the convent's nuns provide an enthusiastic twenty-minute guided tour of the lavishly

▼ ENGELS KLOOSTER

Charles II in Bruges

Charles II of England, who spent three years in exile in Bruges from 1656 to 1659, was an enthusiastic member of the archers' guild and, after the Restoration, he sent them a whopping 3600 florins as a thank you for their hospitality. Charles's enforced exile had begun in 1651 after his attempt to seize the English crown – following the Civil War and the execution of his father in 1649 – had ended in defeat by the Parliamentarians at the Battle of Worcester. Initially, Charles high-tailed it to France, but Cromwell persuaded the French to expel him and the exiled king ended up seeking sanctuary in Spanish territory. He was allowed to settle in Bruges, then part of the Spanish Netherlands, though the Habsburgs were stingy when it came to granting Charles and his retinue an allowance. The royalists were, says a courtier's letter of 1657, "never in greater want... for Englishmen cannot live on bread alone". In addition, Cromwell's spies kept an eagle eye on Charles's activities, filing lurid reports about his conduct. A certain Mr Butler informed Cromwell that "I think I may truly say that greater abominations were never practised among people than at Charles Stuart's court. Fornication, drunkenness and adultery are considered no sins amongst them." It must have made Cromwell's hair stand on end. Cromwell died in 1658 and Charles was informed of this whilst he was playing tennis in Bruges. The message was to the point – "The devil is dead" – and Charles was on the English throne two years later.

decorated Baroque church, whose finest features are the handsome cupola and the altar, an extraordinarily flashy affair made of 23 different types of marble – a gift of the Nithsdales, English aristocrats whose loyalty to the Catholic faith got them into no end of scrapes.

Museum Onze-Lieve-Vrouw ter Potterie (Museum of Our Lady of the Pottery)

Potterierei 79. Tues–Sun 9.30am–12.30pm & 1.30–5pm; €2.50.
The Museum Onze-Lieve-Vrouw ter Potterie was founded as a hospital in the thirteenth century on the site of an earlier pottery – hence the name. The hospital (though "hospital" is a tad misleading, as the buildings were originally used as much to accommodate visitors as tend the sick) was remodelled on several occasions and the three brick gables that front the building today span three centuries. The middle gable is the oldest, dating from 1359 and

built as part of the first hospital chapel. The left-hand gable belonged to the main medieval hospital ward and the one on the right marks a second chapel, added in the 1620s.

Inside, a visit to the museum begins in the former sick room, where a distinctly mediocre selection of medieval religious paintings is partly redeemed by an arresting panel-painting of *St Michael triumphing over the Devil*, by the Master of the St Ursula Legend. Moving on, the museum's chapel is an L-shaped affair distinguished by a sumptuous marble rood screen, whose two side altars recall the museum's location beside what was once one of the city's busiest quays. The altar on the left is dedicated to St Anthony, the patron saint of ships' joiners, the one on the right to St Brendan, the patron saint of seamen. There's also a finely expressed thirteenth-century stone statue of the Virgin on the main altar, but pride of

▲ DE WINDMOLEN

place goes to the set of old tapestries that are hung in the chapel from Easter to October. These comprise a superbly naturalistic, brightly coloured strip cartoon depicting eighteen miracles attributed to Our Lady of the Pottery, almost all to do with being saved from the sea or a sudden change of fortune in fishing or trade. Each carries an inscription, but you'll need to be good at Dutch to decipher them.

Shops

't Apostelientje

Balstraat 11 ℗050 33 78 60. Mon–Sat 9.30am–6pm, Sun 10am–1pm. Close to the Kantcentrum, this small shop sells a charming variety of handmade lace pieces of both modern and traditional design. If there's nothing here that takes your fancy, then try the (even smaller) shop in the Kantcentrum itself.

De Roode Steen

Jan van Eyckplein 8 ℗050 33 61 51. Mon, Tues, Thurs & Fri 10.30am–6pm, Sat & Sun 1–6pm. Occupying a splendid fifteenth-century house on the east side of Jan van Eyckplein, this shop specializes in interior design, with heaps of sumptuous soft furnishings and well-made furniture, as well as smaller items like cushions and lamps. Expensive.

Cafés

De Windmolen

Carmersstraat 135. Mon–Thurs 10am–10pm, Fri & Sun 10am–3pm. This amiable, neighbourhood café-bar, occupying an old brick house at the east end of Carmersstraat, dishes up a decent line in inexpensive snacks and light meals – croque monsieur, spaghetti, lasagne and so forth – and possesses a competent beer menu. Has a pleasant outside terrace and an interior dotted with folksy knick-knacks.

Restaurants

De Karmeliet

Langestraat 19 ℗050 33 82 59, Ⓦwww.dekarmeliet.be. Tues–Sat noon–2pm & 7–9.30pm. Smooth and polished restaurant – one of the city's best – occupying a big, old mansion about five minutes' walk east of the Burg. It's a tad formal for many tastes, but there's no disputing the excellence of the service or the quality of the French cuisine, with an inventive menu featuring dishes like rabbit (*lapin royale*) and marinated cod. À la carte mains from around €40; Reservations essential.

In Den Wittekop

St-Jakobstraat 14 ☎050 33 20 59. Tues–Sat noon–2pm & 6–9.30pm. This small and intimate, split-level restaurant is one of the most appealing in town, its decor a fetching mixture of the tasteful and the kitsch. There's smooth jazz as background music plus good Flemish food, including the local speciality of pork and beef stewed in Trappist beer. Mains average around €18.

Kok au Vin

Ezelstraat 19 ☎050 33 95 21. Mon, Tues & Fri–Sun noon–2pm & 6.30–10pm. Swish restaurant in tastefully modernized old premises on the north side of the city centre. An ambitious menu covers all the Franco-Belgian bases and then some, with mains averaging around €25, though lunch is half that.

Rock Fort

Langestraat 15 ☎050 33 41 13. Mon–Fri noon–2pm & 6.30–11pm. Chic and highly regarded restaurant with a creative, international menu of nouvelle persuasion. Particularly strong on seafood. Main courses average around €20.

't Zonneke

Genthof 5 ☎050 33 07 81. Tues–Sat 12.30–2pm & 6.30–10pm. Cosy restaurant whose modern decor incorporates a few of the premises' original sixteenth-century features. The well-cooked meals include steak and pasta, as well as an ample selection of fish dishes, from around €19.

Bars and clubs

Bistro du Phare

Sasplein 2 ☎050 34 35 90, ⓦwww .duphare.be. Daily except Tues 11.30am till late. Off the beaten track in the northeast corner of the city centre, this busy place offers filling food, a good range of beers and a canal setting. There's also a pleasant summer terrace and evening jazz and blues concerts every month or so – come early to get a seat.

Oud Vlissinghe

Blekersstraat 2 ☎050 34 37 37, ⓦwww.cafevlissinghe.be. Wed–Sat 11am–midnight, Sun 11am–7pm. With its wood panelling, antique paintings and long wooden tables, this is one of the oldest and most distinctive bars in Bruges, thought to date from 1515. The atmosphere is relaxed and easy-going, with the emphasis on quiet conversation – there are no jukeboxes here. There's a pleasant garden terrace, too.

De Republiek

St-Jacobsstraat 36 ☎050 34 02 29, ⓦwww.derepubliek.be. Daily from 11am till 3/4am. One of the most fashionable and popular café-bars in town – though not necessarily the most welcoming staff – with an arty, sometimes alternative and youthful crew. Does very reasonably priced snacks, including vegetarian food and pasta, and has occasional gigs.

De Vuurmolen

Kraanplein 5 ☎050 33 00 79, ⓦwww .vuurmolen.be. Daily 10am–7am. This crowded, youthful bar has a reasonably wide range of beers, a large front terrace and some of the best DJs in town playing a good mix of sounds – techno through house and beyond.

Damme

Now a popular day-trippers' destination, well known for its easy-going atmosphere and clutch of classy restaurants, the quaint village of Damme, 7km north-east of Bruges, was in medieval times the city's main seaport. At its height, it boasted a population of ten thousand souls and guarded the banks of the River Zwin, which gave Bruges direct access to the sea. The river silted up in the late fifteenth century, however, and Damme slipped into a long decline, its old brick buildings rusting away until the tourists and second-homers arrived to create the pretty and genteel village of today.

Damme's one main street, Kerkstraat, is edged by what remains of the medieval town, most memorably the Stadhuis (Town Hall) and the Onze Lieve Vrouwekerk (Church of Our Lady). Kerkstraat also lies at right angles to the pretty, tree-lined canal that links Bruges with Damme and, ultimately, Sluis, a tiny village over the border in Holland. The Sluis canal intersects with the wider and busier Leopoldkanaal just 2km to the northeast of Damme, and together they frame a delightfully scenic sliver of countryside dotted with whitewashed farmhouses and patterned by old causeways − perfect for cycling.

The Stadhuis (Town Hall)

Kerkstraat. Not open to the public.
Funded by a special tax on barrels of herrings, the fifteenth-century Stadhuis, just a few steps down Kerkstraat from the Sluis canal, is easily the best looking building in the village, its elegant, symmetrical facade balanced by the graceful lines of its exterior stairway. In one of the niches you'll spy Charles the Bold offering a wedding ring to Margaret of York, who stands in the next niche along − appropriately enough, as the couple got spliced here in Damme, a prestige event that attracted aristocratic bigwigs from all over western Europe.

▼ CANAL NEAR DAMME

▲ THE STADHUIS, DAMME

Flanders, so he became more of a scoundrel than a joker until, that is, the Belgian Charles de Coster (1827–79) subverted the legend, turning Ulenspiegel into the enemy of King Philip II of Spain and the embodiment of the Belgian hankering for freedom. Coster made Damme the home of Ulenspiegel, who was accompanied by his fiancée Nele and his loyal chum Lamme Goedzak.

St Janshospitaal

Kerkstraat. April–Sept Mon & Fri 2–6pm, Tues–Thurs, Sat & Sun 11am–noon & 2–6pm; €1.50. Just down the street from the Stadhuis, St Janshospitaal accommodates a small museum of five rooms and a dainty little chapel. Room 1 houses a couple of curiously crude parchment-and-straw peasants' pictures of St Peter and St Paul, while rooms 2 and 3 have some fine old furniture. Room 4, the main room, displays an enjoyable sample of Delftware and pewter,

Tijl Ulenspiegel Museum

Jacob van Maerlantstraat 3. Mon–Fri 9am–noon & 2–5pm, Sat & Sun 10am–noon & 2–5pm; mid-April to mid-Oct until 6pm; €2.50. Metres from the Stadhuis, the Tijl Ulenspiegel Museum is devoted to the eponymous folkloric figure who started out as a fool-cum-prankster in Germany in the fourteenth century. As Ulenspiegel stories spread into

Arrival and information

There are several ways of reaching Damme from Bruges, the most rewarding being the seven-kilometre cycle ride out along the tree-lined Brugge–Sluis canal, which begins at the Dampoort, on the northeast edge of the city centre. Cycle rental is available in Bruges (see p.155) and in Damme at Tijl en Nele, round the corner from the Stadhuis at Jacob van Maerlantstraat 2 (reservations advised; ☏050 35 71 92; closed Wed; €10 per day).

You can also get from Bruges to Damme by canal boat, with excursions starting about 500m east of the Dampoort on the Noorweegse Kaai (Easter to mid-Oct 5 daily each way; 40min; one-way €5.20, return €6.70); tickets are purchased on board. Connecting bus #4 from the Markt and the bus station, next to the train station, runs to the Noorweegse Kaai to meet most departures – but check at the De Lijn information kiosk, outside the train station, before you set out.

Finally, you can reach Damme on city bus #43 from the bus station or the Markt (April–Sept 6 daily each way; 20min). During the rest of the year, the bus runs less frequently and you'll be forced to hang around for longer than you'll want in Damme – if, indeed, you can make the return journey at all.

Damme has its own tourist office, across the street from the Stadhuis at Jacob van Maerlantstraat 3 (Mon–Fri 9am–noon & 2–5pm, Sat & Sun 10am–noon & 2–5pm; mid-April to mid-Oct until 6pm; ☏050 28 86 10, ⓦwww.toerismedamme.be).

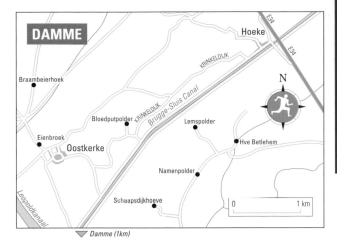

▽ *Damme (1km)*

but it's the chimneypiece that grabs the attention, a Baroque extravagance with a cast-iron back-plate representing the penance of King David for the murder of Bathsheba's husband. Otherwise, the museum holds a mildly diverting assortment of liturgical objects, a potpourri of ceramic ware and folksy votive offerings.

Onze Lieve Vrouwekerk (Church of Our Lady)

Kerkstraat. May–Sept daily 10.30am–noon & 2.30–5.30pm; €1. From St Janshospitaal, it's a couple of minutes' walk further down Kerkstraat to the Onze Lieve Vrouwekerk, a sturdy brick structure in classic Gothic style. The church is attached to a ruined segment of the original nave (open access) that speaks volumes about Damme's decline: the church was built in the thirteenth century, but when the population shrank it was just too big and so the inhabitants abandoned part of the nave and the remnants are now stuck between the present church and its clumpy

tower. Climb the tower for panoramic views over the surrounding polders. The large and enigmatic, three-headed modern statue beside the tower is the work of the contemporary Belgian painter and sculptor Charles Delporte.

Just beyond the church, on the right hand side of Kerkstraat a footpath branches off along a narrow canal to loop round the west side of Damme, an enjoyable ten minute stroll through the poplars which brings you out just west of the village beside the Brugge–Sluis canal.

Cycling around Damme

Damme lies at the start of a pretty little parcel of land, a rural backwater crisscrossed by drowsy canals and causeways, each of which is shadowed by two long lines of slender poplar trees which quiver and rustle in the prevailing westerly winds. This perfect cycling country extends as far as the €34 motorway, about 6km from Damme. There are lots of possible cycling routes and, if you want to explore the area in detail, you should buy the detailed, 1:50,000 Fietsnetwerk Brugse Ommeland Noord cycling map (€6; available from any major bookstore or the Bruges tourist office) before you set out.

One especially rewarding itinerary, taking in some of the most charming scenery hereabouts, is a fifteen-kilometre round-trip that begins by leaving Damme to the northeast along the Brugge–Sluis canal, then crosses over the Leopoldkanaal before continuing along the canal to the hamlet of Hoeke. Here, just over the bridge, turn hard left for the narrow causeway – the Krinkeldijk – that wanders straight back in the direction of Damme, running to the north of the Brugge–Sluis canal. Just over 3km long, the causeway drifts across a beguiling landscape of bright whitewashed farmhouses and deep-green

▲ SIGNS NEAR DAMME

The Battle of Damme

In the summer of 1340, a French fleet assembled in the estuary of the River Zwin to prepare for an invasion of England. To combat the threat the English king, Edward III, sailed across the Channel and attacked at dawn. Although they were outnumbered three to one, Edward's fleet won an extraordinary victory, his bowmen causing chaos by showering the French ships with arrows from a safe distance. A foretaste of the Battle of Crecy, there was so little left of the French force that no one dared tell King Philip VI of France, until finally the court jester took matters into his own hands: "Oh! The English cowards! They had not the courage to jump into the sea as our noble Frenchmen did." Philip's reply is not recorded.

grassy fields before reaching an intersection where you turn left to regain the Brugge–Sluis waterway.

Shops

AHA

Kerkstraat 24 ☎050 54 85 47. Easter to Sept daily 11am–6pm, Fri from 1.30pm; Oct to Easter Tues–Sun 1.30–6pm. Cosy little bookshop with a good section on tourist attractions in Bruges and its immediate surroundings. Sells comics, too.

Diogenes

Kerkstraat 22. July & Aug daily 11am–6pm; Sept–June Sat & Sun 11am–6pm. Pocket-sized antiquarian bookshop focusing on literature and art, with many English titles.

Cafés and restaurants

Bij Lamme Goedzak

Kerkstraat 13 ☎050 35 20 03. April–Sept daily except Thurs 11am–10pm; Oct–March Mon–Fri noon–2pm, Sat & Sun 11am–10pm. The best restaurant in Damme, serving snacks and light meals during the day and mouth-watering traditional Flemish

dishes, often featuring wild game, in the evening, when main courses run at about €25. Also sells its own house ales and has a garden terrace at the back and a pavement terrace at the front.

Restaurant De Lieve

Jacob van Maerlantstraat 10 ☎050 35 66 30. Wed–Sun 6–10pm. Just behind the Stadhuis, this smart and formal restaurant offers the best of Flemish and French cuisine, with mains from €22.

Tante Marie Pâtisserie

Kerkstraat 38. Daily except Fri 10am–7pm. Pleasant, modern pâtisserie and tea room selling tasty light meals and the best cakes and pastries in town.

▼ BIJ LAMME GOEDZAK

Central Ghent

Ghent may be more of a sprawl and less immediately picturesque than Bruges, its great and ancient rival, but it still musters a string of superb Gothic buildings and a bevy of delightful, intimate streetscapes, where antique brick houses are woven around a skein of narrow canals. The city's star turn is undoubtedly St Baafskathedraal, home to Jan van Eyck's remarkable Adoration of the Mystic Lamb, but it's well-supported by a clutch of other attractions including exquisite medieval guildhouses, enjoyable museums and a regiment of lively bars and first-class restaurants. But perhaps most importantly, Ghent remains a quintes-sentially Flemish city with a tourist industry – rather than the other way round – and if you find the tourists and tweeness of Bruges a tad overpowering, this is the place to decamp, just twenty minutes away by train.

Like Bruges, Ghent prospered throughout the Middle Ages, but it also suffered from endemic disputes between the count and his nobles (who supported France) and the cloth-reliant citizens (to whom friendship with England was vital). Unlike Bruges, however, Ghent experienced an industrial boom in the nineteenth century and remains first and foremost

A **museum pass**, valid for three days and covering fourteen of the city's sights and museums, costs just €12.50. It's available at any of the fourteen places included, as well as from the tourist office (see p.155) and some hotels.

an industrial city, Belgium's third largest. Many of Ghent's fine old

▼ CENTRAL GHENT

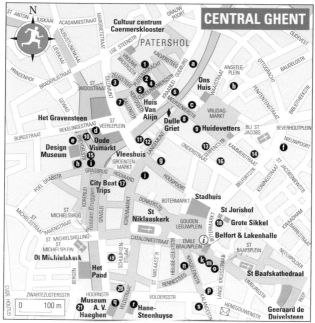

CENTRAL GHENT

buildings took a battering as the city focused on industry, but in the last twenty years its ancient centre has benefited from an extraordinarily ambitious programme of restoration and refurbishment which has cleared away the accumulated grime.

The shape and structure of the city centre reflects Ghent's ancient class and linguistic divide. The streets to the south of the Korenmarkt (Corn Market), by St Niklaaskerk, the traditional focus of the city, tend to be

straight and wide, lined with elegant old mansions, the former habitations of the wealthier, French-speaking classes, while, to the north, Flemish Ghent is all narrow alleys and low brick houses. The two areas meet at the somewhat confusing sequence of squares that spread east from the Korenmarkt to St Baafskathedraal.

St Baafskathedraal

St Bavo's Cathedral, St Baafsplein.
Daily: April–Oct 8.30am–6pm;
Nov–March 8.30am–5pm; free.

Walking tours and boat trips

Guided **walking tours** are particularly popular in Ghent. The standard walking tour, organized by the tourist office, comprises a two-hour jaunt round the city centre (May–Oct daily at 2.30pm; Nov–April Sat at 2.30pm; €7); advance booking – at least a few hours ahead of time – is strongly recommended. Alternatively, horse-drawn carriages line up outside the Lakenhalle, on St Baafsplein, offering a thirty-minute canter round town for €25 (April–Oct daily 10am–6pm & most winter weekends).

Throughout the year, **boat trips** explore Ghent's inner waterways, departing from the Korenlei and Graslei quays, near the Korenmarkt, as well as from the Vleeshuisbrug, metres from the Groentenmarkt (March to mid-Nov daily 10am–6pm; mid-Nov to Feb Sat & Sun 11am–4pm; €6). Trips last forty minutes and leave roughly every fifteen minutes, though the wait can be longer as boats often only leave when reasonably full.

The best place to start an exploration of the city is the mainly Gothic St Baafskathedraal, squeezed into the eastern corner of St Baafsplein and named after a local seventh-century landowner turned Christian missionary. The third church on this site, and two hundred and fifty years in the making, the cathedral is a tad lop-sided, but there's no gainsaying the imposing beauty of the west tower, with its long, elegant windows and perky corner turrets. Some 82m high, the tower was the last major part of the church to be completed, topped off in 1554 – just before the outbreak of the religious wars that were to wrack the country for the next one hundred years.

Inside the cathedral, the chapel displaying *The Adoration of the Mystic Lamb* (see opposite) is on the left at the beginning of the mighty fifteenth-century nave, whose tall, slender columns give the whole interior a cheerful sense of lightness, though the Baroque marble screen spoils the effect by darkening the choir. In the nave, the principal item of interest is the rococo pulpit, a whopping oak and marble affair, where

the main timber represents the Tree of Life with an allegorical representation of Time and Truth at its base. Beyond, the high altar, with its tons of marble, features an enthroned St Baaf ascending to heaven on an untidy heap of clouds, whilst the neighbouring north transept holds a characteristically energetic painting by Rubens (1577–1640) entitled *St Baaf entering the Abbey of Ghent*. Dating to 1624, it includes a self-portrait – he's the bearded head. Also in the north transept is the entrance to the dank and capacious vaulted crypt, a survivor from the earlier Romanesque church. The crypt is stuffed with religious bric-a-brac of some mild interest, but the highlight is Justus van Gent's superb fifteenth-century triptych, *The Crucifixion of Christ*. This depicts the crucified Christ flanked, on the left, by Moses purifying the waters of Mara with wood, and to the right by Moses and the bronze serpent which cured poisoned Israelites on sight. As the Bible has it: "So Moses made a bronze serpent [as the Lord had commanded] and set it on a pole; and if a serpent bit any man, he would look at the bronze serpent and live".

The Adoration of the Mystic Lamb

Daily: April–Oct Mon–Sat 9.30am–5pm, Sun 1–5pm; Nov–March Mon–Sat 10.30am–4pm, Sun 1–4pm; €3.

In a small side chapel to the left of the cathedral entrance is Ghent's greatest treasure, a winged altarpiece known as *The Adoration of the Mystic Lamb* (*De Aanbidding van het Lam Gods*), a seminal work of the early 1430s, though of dubious provenance. Since the discovery of a Latin verse on its frame in the nineteenth century, academics have been arguing about who actually painted it. The inscription reads that Hubert van Eyck "than whom none was greater" began, and Jan van Eyck, "second in art", completed the work, but as nothing else is known of Hubert, some art historians doubt his existence. They argue that Jan, who lived and worked in several cities, including Ghent, was entirely responsible for the painting and that only later, after Jan had firmly rooted himself in the rival city of Bruges, did the citizens

of Ghent invent "Hubert" to counter his fame. No one knows the altarpiece's authorship for sure, but what is certain is that in his manipulation of the technique of oil painting the artist – or artists – was able to capture a needle-sharp, luminous realism that must have stunned their contemporaries.

The altarpiece is now displayed with its panels open, though originally these were kept closed and the painting only revealed on high days and holidays. Consequently, it's actually best to begin round the back with the cover screens, which hold a beautiful **Annunciation scene** with the archangel Gabriel's wings reaching up to the timbered ceiling of a Flemish house, the streets of a town visible through the windows. In a brilliant coup of lighting, the shadows of the angel dapple the room, emphasizing the reality of the apparition – a technique repeated on the opposite cover panel around the figure of Mary. Below, the donor and his wife, a certain Joos Vydt and Isabella Borlout, kneel piously alongside statues of the saints.

▼ THE ADORATION OF THE MYSTIC LAMB

By design, the restrained exterior was but a foretaste of what lies within – a striking, visionary work of art whose brilliant colours and precise draughtsmanship still takes the breath away. On the **upper level** sit God the Father (some say Christ Triumphant), the Virgin and John the Baptist in gleaming clarity; to the right are musician-angels and a nude, pregnant Eve; and on the left is Adam plus a group of singing angels, who strain to read their music. The celebrated, sixteenth-century Flemish art critic Karel van Mander argued that the singers were so artfully painted that he could discern the different pitches of their voices – and, true or not, it is the detail that impresses, especially the richly embroidered trimmings on the cloaks.

In the **lower central panel** the Lamb, the symbol of Christ's sacrifice, is depicted in a heavenly paradise – "the first evolved landscape in European painting", suggested Kenneth Clark – seen as a sort of idealized Low Countries. The Lamb stands on an altar whose rim is minutely inscribed with a quotation from the Gospel of St John, "Behold the Lamb of God, which taketh away the sins of the world". Four groups converge on the Lamb from the corners of the central panel. In the bottom right are a group of male saints and up above them are their female equivalents; the bottom left shows the patriarchs of the Old Testament and above them are an assortment of bishops, dressed in blue vestments and carrying palm branches.

On the **side panels**, approaching the Lamb across symbolically rough and stony ground, are more saintly figures.

On the right-hand side are two groups, the first being St Anthony and his hermits, the second St Christopher, shown here as a giant with a band of pilgrims. On the left side panel come the horsemen, the inner group symbolizing the Warriors of Christ – including St George bearing a shield with a red cross – and the outer the Just Judges, each of whom is dressed in fancy Flemish attire. The Just Judges panel is not, however, authentic. It was added during the 1950s to replace the original, which was stolen in 1934 and never recovered. The lost panel features in Albert Camus's novel *The Fall*, whose protagonist keeps it in a cupboard, declining to return it for a complex of reasons, one of which is "because those judges are on their way to meet the Lamb ... [but] ... there is no lamb or innocence any longer". Naturally enough, there has been endless speculation as to who stole the panel and why with suspicion ultimately resting on a certain Arsène Goedertier, a stockbroker and conservative politician from just outside of Ghent, who made a deathbed confession in 1934. Whether he was acting alone or as an agent for others is still hotly contested – some argue that the theft was orchestrated by the Knights Templar (ridiculous), others by the Nazis (much more likely), but no-one really knows.

The theft was just one of many dramatic events to befall the painting – indeed it's remarkable that the altarpiece has survived at all. The Calvinists wanted to destroy it; Philip II of Spain tried to acquire it; the Emperor Joseph II disapproved of the painting so violently that he replaced the nude Adam

and Eve with a clothed version in 1784 (exhibited today on a column at the start of the nave just inside the church entrance); and near the end of World War II the Germans hid it in an Austrian salt mine, where it remained until American soldiers arrived in 1945.

The Lakenhalle (Cloth Hall)

St Baafsplein. Across from the cathedral, on the west side of St Baafsplein, lurks the Lakenhalle, a dour hunk of a building with an unhappy history. Work began on the hall in the early fifteenth century, but the cloth trade slumped before it was finished and it was only grudgingly completed in 1903. No one has ever quite worked out what to do with the building ever since, and today it's little more than an empty shell with the city's tourist office tucked away in the basement on the north side. This basement was long used as the town prison, whose entrance was round on the west side of the Lakenhalle through the Mammelokker (The Suckling), a grandiose Louis XIV-style portal that stands propped up against the main body of the building. Part gateway and part warder's lodging, the Mammelokker was added in 1741 and is adorned by a bas-relief sculpture illustrating the classical legend of Cimon, who the Romans condemned to death by starvation. He was saved by his daughter, Pero, who turned up daily to feed him from her breasts – hence the name.

The Belfort (Belfry)

St Baafsplein. Mid-March to mid-Nov daily 10am–6pm; €3. The first-floor entrance on the south side of the Lakenhalle is the

▲ THE BELFORT

only way to reach the adjoining Belfort, a much-amended medieval edifice whose soaring spire is topped by a comically corpulent, gilded copper dragon. Once a watchtower-cum-storehouse for civic documents, the interior is now just an empty shell displaying a few old bells and statues alongside the rusting remains of a couple of old dragons which formerly perched on top of the spire. The belfry is equipped with a glass-sided lift that climbs up to the roof, where consolation is provided in the form of excellent views out over the city centre.

The Stadhuis (Town Hall)

Botermarkt. Entrance by guided tour only (May–Oct Mon–Thurs daily at 2.30pm) as the first 45min of the 2hr walking tour organized by the tourist office (see p.155); full 2hr tour €7, Stadhuis only €4. Stretching along the west side of the Botermarkt, just to the north of the Lakenhalle, is the striking, recently restored Stadhuis. The building's main facade comprises two distinct sections. The later section, framing the central stairway, dates from the 1580s

▲ COAT OF ARMS, STADHUIS

and offers a good example of Italian Renaissance architecture, its crisp symmetries faced by a multitude of black-painted columns. In stark contrast are the wild, curling patterns of the section to the immediate north, carved in Flamboyant Gothic style at the turn of the sixteenth century to a design by one of the era's most celebrated architects, Rombout Keldermans (1460–1531). The whole of the Stadhuis was originally to have been built by Keldermans, but the money ran out when the wool trade collapsed and the city couldn't afford to finish it off until much later – hence today's discordant facade. Look carefully at Keldermans' work and you'll spot all sorts of charming details, especially in the elaborate tracery, decorated with oak leaves and acorns as well as vines laden with grapes. Each one of the ornate niches was intended to hold a statuette, but Keldermans never quite got round to them and the present carvings, representing important historical personages in characteristic poses, were added in the nineteenth century.

Inside the Stadhuis, guided tours amble round a series of halls and chambers, the most interesting being the old Court of Justice or Pacificatiezaal (Pacification Hall), where the Pacification of Ghent treaty was signed in 1576. A plaque commemorates this agreement, which momentarily bound the rebel armies of the Low Countries (today's Belgium and The Netherlands) together against their rulers, the Spanish Habsburgs. The carrot offered by the dominant Protestants was the promise of religious freedom, but they failed to deliver and much of the south (present-day Belgium) soon returned to the Spanish fold. The hall's charcoal and cream tiled floor is designed in the form of a maze. No one's quite certain why, but it's supposed that more privileged felons (or sinners) had to struggle round the maze on their knees as a substitute punishment for a pilgrimage to Jerusalem – a good deal if ever there was one.

St Niklaaskerk

Emile Braunplein. Mon 2–5pm, Tues–Sun 10am–5pm; free.
Southwest of the Stadhuis, St Niklaaskerk is an architectural hybrid, dating from the thirteenth century, which was once the favourite church of the city's wealthier merchants. It's the shape and structure that pleases most, especially the arching buttresses and pencil-thin turrets which, in a classic example of the early Scheldt Gothic style, elegantly attenuate the lines of the nave. Inside, many of the Baroque furnishings and fittings have been removed and the windows un-bricked, thus returning the church to its early appearance, though unfortunately this

does not apply to a clumsy and clichéd set of statues of the apostles. Much better is the giant-sized Baroque high altar with its mammoth representation of God the Father glowering down its back, blowing the hot wind of the Last Judgement from his mouth and surrounded by a flock of cherubic angels. The church is sometimes used for temporary art exhibitions, which can attract an admission fee.

▲ ST NIKLAASKERK

The Korenmarkt

St Niklaaskerk marks the southern end of the Korenmarkt (Corn Market), a long and wide cobbled area where the grain that once kept the city alive was traded after it was unloaded on the neighbouring Graslei dock (see below). The one noteworthy building here is the former post office, whose combination of Gothic Revival and neo-Renaissance styles illustrates the eclecticism popular in Belgium at the beginning of the twentieth century. The carved heads encircling the building represent the rulers who came to the city for the Great Exhibition of 1913; among them, curiously enough, is a bust of Florence Nightingale. The interior is now a shopping mall.

St Michielsbrug

Behind the post office, the neo-Gothic St Michielsbrug (St Michael's Bridge) offers fine views back over the towers and turrets that pierce the Ghent skyline – just as it was meant to: the bridge was built to provide visitors to the Great Exhibition with a vantage point from which to admire the city centre. As such, it was one of several schemes dreamed up to enhance Ghent's medieval appearance, one of the others being the demolition of the scrabbly buildings that had sprung up in the lee of the Lakenhalle. The bridge also overlooks the city's oldest harbour, the Tussen Bruggen (Between the Bridges), from whose quays – the Korenlei and the Graslei – boats leave for trips around the city's canals (see box, p.110).

The guild houses of the Graslei

Ghent's boatmen and grainweighers were crucial to the functioning of the medieval city, and they built a row of splendid guild houses along the Graslei, each gable decorated with an appropriate sign or symbol. Working your way north from St Michielsbrug, the first building of distinction is the Gildehuis van de Vrije Schippers (Guild House of the Free Boatmen), at no. 14, where the badly weathered sandstone is decorated with scenes of boatmen weighing anchor, plus a delicate carving of a caravel – the type of Mediterranean sailing ship used by Columbus – located above the door. Medieval Ghent had two boatmen guilds: the Free, who could discharge their cargoes within the city, and the Unfree, who could not. The Unfree Boatmen were obliged to unload their goods into the vessels of the Free Boatmen at the edge of the city – an inefficient arrangement by any standard, though typical of the complex regulations governing the guilds.

Next door, at nos. 12–13, the seventeenth-century Cooremetershuys (Corn Measurers' House) was where city officials weighed and graded corn behind a facade graced by cartouches and garlands of fruit. Next to this, at no. 11, stands the quaint Tolhuisje, another delightful example of Flemish Renaissance architecture, built to house the customs officers in 1698, while the adjacent limestone Spijker (Staple House), at no. 10, boasts a surly Romanesque facade dating from around 1200. It was here that the city stored its grain supply for over five hundred years until a fire gutted the interior. Finally, three doors down at no. 8, the splendid Den Enghel takes its name from the angel bearing a banner that decorates the facade; the building was originally the stonemasons' guild house, as evidenced by the effigies of the four Roman martyrs who were the guild's patron saints, though they are depicted in medieval attire rather than togas and sandals.

The Groentenmarkt

Just north of Graslei, on the far side of Hooiard street, is the Groentenmarkt (Vegetable Market), one of the city's prettier squares, a jumble of old buildings which house one especially distinctive shop, Tierenteyn, the mustard specialist (see p.125). The west side of the square is flanked by a long line of sooty stone gables which were once the retaining walls of the Groot Vleeshuis (Great Butchers' Hall), a covered market in which meat was sold under the careful control of the city council. The gables date from the fifteenth century but are in poor condition and the interior is only of interest for its intricate wooden roof.

The Korenlei

From the north end of Graslei, the Grasbrug bridge leads over to the Korenlei, which trips along the western

▲ CARVING OF CARAVEL GUILD HOUSE OF THE FREE BOATMEN

▲ DESIGN MUSEUM

side of the old city harbour. Unlike the Graslei opposite, none of the medieval buildings have survived here and instead there's a series of expansive, high-gabled Neoclassical merchants' houses, mostly dating from the eighteenth century. It's the general ensemble that appeals rather than any particular building, but the Gildehuis van de Onvrije Schippers (Guild House of the Unfree Boatmen), at no.7, does boast a fetching eighteenth-century façade decorated with whimsical dolphins and bewigged lions, all bulging eyes and rows of teeth.

St Michielskerk

Onderbergen. April–Sept Mon–Sat 2–5pm; free. At the south end of Korenlei, on the far side of St Michielsbrug, rises the bulky mass of St Michielskerk, a heavy-duty Gothic structure begun in the 1440s. The city's Protestants seem to have taken a particularly strong disliking to the place, ransacking it twice – once in 1566 and again in 1579 – and the repairs were never quite finished, as witnessed by the forlorn and clumsily truncated tower. Entered on Onderbergen, the interior is, however, much more enticing, the broad sweep of the five-aisled nave punctuated

by tall and slender columns that shoot up to the arching vaults of the roof. Most of the furnishings and fittings are Gothic Revival, pedestrian stuff enlivened by a scattering of sixteenth- and seventeenth-century paintings, the pick of which is a splendidly impassioned *Crucifixion* by Anthony van Dyck (1599–1641) in the north transept. Trained in Antwerp, where he worked in Rubens' workshop, van Dyck made extended visits to England and Italy in the 1620s, before returning to Antwerp in 1628. He stayed there for four years – during which time he painted this *Crucifixion* – before migrating to England to become portrait painter to Charles I and his court.

The Design Museum

Jan Breydelstraat 5. Tues–Sun 10am–6pm; €2.50; @www .designmuseumgent.be. At the north end of Korenlei is the Design Museum, one of the city's more enjoyable museums, which focuses on Belgian decorative and applied arts. The wide-ranging collection divides into two distinct sections. At the front, squeezed into what was once an eighteenth-century patrician's mansion, is an attractive sequence of period rooms, mostly illustrating the Baroque and

PLACES

Central Ghent

▲ HET GRAVENSTEEN

the Rococo. The original dining room is especially fine, from its fancy painted ceiling and ornate Chinese porcelain to its elaborate wooden chandelier and intricately carved elm panelling.

The second section, at the back of the mansion, comprises a gleamingly modern display area used both for temporary exhibitions and to showcase the museum's eclectic collection of applied arts dating from 1880 to the present day. There are examples of the work of many leading designers, but the Art Nouveau material is perhaps the most visually arresting, especially the finely crafted furnishings of the Belgian Henry van der Velde (1863–1957).

Het Gravensteen

St Veerleplein. Daily: April–Sept 9am–5/6pm; Oct–March 9am–4/5pm; €6. At the top of Jan Breydelstraat, turn right and cross the bridge to reach Het Gravensteen, the castle of the counts of Flanders, which looks sinister enough to have been lifted from a Bosch painting. Its cold, dark walls and unyielding turrets were first raised in 1180 as much to intimidate the town's unruly citizens as to protect them and,

considering the castle has been used for all sorts of purposes since then (it was even used as a cotton mill), it has survived in remarkably good nick. The imposing gateway comprises a deep-arched, heavily fortified tunnel leading to the courtyard, which is framed by protective battlements complete with wooden flaps, ancient arrow slits and apertures for boiling oil and water.

Overlooking the courtyard stand the castle's two main buildings: the count's residence on the left and the keep on the right, each riddled with narrow, interconnected staircases set within the thickness of the walls. A self-guided tour takes you through this labyrinth, the first highlight being a room full of medieval military hardware, from suits of armour, pikes, swords and daggers through to an exquisitely crafted sixteenth-century crossbow. Beyond is a gruesome collection of instruments of torture, the count's cavernous state rooms and a particularly dank, underground dungeon (an oubliette). It's also possible to walk along most of the castle's encircling wall, from where there are pleasing views over the city centre.

St Veerleplein and the Oude Vismarkt

Public punishments ordered by the counts and countesses of Flanders were carried out in front of the castle on St Veerleplein, now an attractive cobbled square with an ersatz punishment post, plonked here in 1913 and topped off by a lion carrying the banner of Flanders. At the back of the square, beside the junction of the city's two main canals, is the grandiloquent Baroque facade of the Oude Vismarkt (Old Fish Market), in which Neptune stands on a chariot drawn by sea horses. To either side are allegorical figures representing the River Leie (Venus) and the River Scheldt (Hercules) – the two rivers that spawned the city. The market itself is in a terrible state, scheduled for restoration – or possibly demolition.

Huis van Alijn Museum

Kraanlei 65. Tues–Sat 11am–5pm, Sun 10am–5pm; €2.50; www.huisvanalijn.be. A short stroll east of St Veerleplein is one of the city's more popular attractions, the Huis van Alijn, a folklore museum which occupies a series of exceptionally pretty little almshouses set around a central courtyard. Dating from the fourteenth century, the almshouses were built following a major scandal reminiscent of *Romeo and Juliet*. In 1354, two members of the Rijms family murdered three of the rival Alijns when they were at Mass in St Baafskathedraal. The immediate cause of the affray was rivalry between members of the families over the same woman, but the dispute went deeper, reflecting the commercial animosity of two guilds, the weavers and the fullers. The murderers fled for their lives and were condemned to death in absentia, but were eventually – eight years later – pardoned on condition that they paid for the construction of a set of almshouses, which was to be named after the victims. The result was the Huis van Alijn, which became a hospice for elderly women and then a workers' tenement until the city council snapped it up in the 1950s.

The **museum** consists of two sets of period rooms depicting local life and work in the eighteenth and nineteenth centuries, one each on either side of the central courtyard. The duller rooms hold reconstructed shops and workshops – a dispensary, a cobbler's and so forth – the more interesting are thematic, illustrating particular aspects of traditional Flemish society. There are, for example, good displays on funerals and death, popular entertainment – from brass bands through to sports and fairs – and on religious beliefs in an age when every ailment had its own allocated saint. The more substantial exhibits are explained in free multilingual leaflets, which are available in the appropriate room, but generally the labelling is very skimpy. One of the rooms on the right hand side of the museum has a bank of miniature TV screens showing short, locally made amateur films in a continuous cycle. Some of these date back to the 1920s, but most are post-war including a snippet featuring a local 1970s soccer team in terrifyingly tight shorts.

Overlooking the central courtyard in between the two

sets of period rooms is the **chapel**, a pleasantly gaudy affair built in the 1540s and now decorated with folksy shrines and votive offerings. When they aren't out on loan, the chapel is also home to a pair of "goliaths", large and fancily dressed wooden figures that are a common feature of Belgian street processions and festivals.

Along Kraanlei

Pushing on along Kraanlei from the Huis van Alijn Museum, it's only a few paces more to two especially fine facades. First up, at no.79, is De Zeven Werken van Barmhartigheid (The Seven Works of Mercy), a building which takes its name from the miniature panels which decorate its front. The panels on the top level, from left to right, illustrate the mercies of visiting the sick, ministering to prisoners and burying the dead, whilst those below (again from left to right) show feeding the hungry, providing water for the thirsty, and clothing the naked. The seventh good work – giving shelter to the stranger – was provided inside the building, which was once an inn, so, perhaps rather too subtly, there's no decorative panel.

The adjacent Fluitspeler (The Flautist), the corner house at no. 81, dates from 1669 and is now occupied by a restaurant. The six bas-relief terracotta panels on this facade sport allegorical representations of the five senses plus a flying deer; above, on the cornice, are the figures of Faith, Hope and Charity.

The Patershol and Provinciaal Cultuurcentrum Caermersklooster

Behind Kraanlei are the lanes and alleys of the Patershol, a tight web of brick terraced houses dating from the seventeenth century. Once the heart of the Flemish working-class city, this thriving residential quarter had, by the 1970s, become a slum threatened with demolition. After much to-ing and fro-ing, the area was saved from the developers and a process of gentrification begun, the result being today's gaggle of good bars and smashing restaurants. The process is still under way and the fringes of the Patershol remain a ragbag of decay and restoration, but few Belgian cities can boast a more agreeable drinking and eating district.

One specific sight here is the grand old Carmelite Monastery on Vrouwebroersstraat, now the Provinciaal Cultuurcentrum Caermersklooster (℡09 269 29 10, Ⓦwww.caermersklooster .be), which showcases temporary exhibitions of contemporary art, photography, design and fashion.

Dulle Griet

At the north end of Kraanlei, an antiquated little bridge leads over to Dulle Griet (Mad Meg), a lugubrious fifteenth-century cannon whose failure to fire provoked a bitter row between Ghent and the nearby Flemish town of Oudenaarde, where it was cast. In the 1570s, fearful of a Habsburg attack, Ghent purchased the cannon from Oudenaarde. As the region's most powerful siege gun, able to propel a 340kg cannon ball several hundred metres, it seemed a good buy, but when Ghent's gunners tried it out the barrel cracked on first firing and, much to the chagrin of Ghent's city council, Oudenaarde refused to offer a refund. The useless lump was

▲ ARTEVELDE STATUE

on each other in a riot that cost 500 lives – a day that was subsequently entered on the civic calendar as Kwade Maandag (Wicked Monday). In the middle of the square stands a nineteenth-century statue of the guild leader Jacob van Artevelde (see box below), portrayed addressing the people in heroic style.

Of the buildings flanking the Vrijdagmarkt, the most appealing is the former Gildehuis van de Huidevetters (Tanners' Guild House), at no.37, a tall, Gothic structure whose pert dormer windows and stepped gables culminate in a dainty and distinctive corner turret – the Toreken. Also worth a second glance is the old headquarters of the trade unions, the whopping Ons Huis (Our House), a sterling edifice built in eclectic style at the turn of the twentieth century.

Adjoining Vrijdagmarkt is busy Bij St Jacobs, a sprawling square sprinkled with antique shops and set around a sulky medieval church. The square hosts the city's biggest and best flea market (*prondelmarkt*) on Fridays, Saturdays and Sundays from 8am to 1pm.

then rolled to the edge of the Vrijdagmarkt, where it has stayed ever since.

The Vrijdagmarkt and Bij St Jacobs

From Dulle Griet, it's only a few metres to the Vrijdagmarkt, a wide square that was long the political centre of Ghent, the site of both public meetings and executions – and sometimes both at the same time. It was here, too, at the sound of the bells, that the guildsmen gathered whenever their rights were infringed, though on one occasion, on May 2, 1345, the fullers and the weavers turned

Jacob van Artevelde

One of the shrewdest of Ghent's medieval leaders, Jacob van Artevelde (1290–1345) was elected captain of all the guilds in 1337. Initially, he steered a delicate course during the interminable wars between France and England, keeping the city neutral – and the textile industry going – despite the machinations of both warring countries. Ultimately, however, he was forced to take sides, plumping for England. This proved his undoing: in a burst of Anglomania, Artevelde rashly suggested that a son of Edward III of England become the new Count of Flanders, an unpopular notion that prompted a mob to storm his house and hack him to death.

Artevelde's demise fuelled further outbreaks of communal violence and, a few weeks later, the Vrijdagmarkt witnessed a riot between the fullers and the weavers that left five hundred dead. This rumbling vendetta – one of several that plagued the city – was the backdrop to the creation of the Huis van Alijn (see p.119).

St Jorishof

Commonly known as
St Jorishof, the building facing
the Stadhuis, on the corner of
Botermarkt and Hoogpoort,
is one of the city's oldest, its
heavy-duty stonework dating
from the middle of the fifteenth
century. This was once the
home of the Crossbowmen's
Guild, and although the
crossbow was a dead military
duck by the time it was built,
the guild was still a powerful
political force – and remained
so until the eighteenth century.
It was here, in 1477, that Mary
of Burgundy (see p.71) was
pressured into signing the
Great Privilege confirming the
city's commercial freedoms.
She was obviously not too
offended as later that year this
was where she chose to receive
the matrimonial ambassadors
of the Holy Roman Emperor,
Frederick III. Frederick
was pressing the suit of his
son, Maximilian, who Mary
duly married, the end result
being that Flanders became a
Habsburg fiefdom.

Hoogpoort

Lining up along the
Hoogpoort, beyond St Jorishof,
are some of the oldest facades
in Ghent, sturdy if sooty
Gothic structures dating from
the fifteenth century. The
third house along – formerly
a heavily protected aristocratic
mansion called the Grote
Sikkel – is now the home of a
music school, but the blackened
remains of an antique torch-
snuffer remain fixed to the wall
beside the grand double doors.

Geeraard de Duivelsteen

Reep. No admission. Southeast of
St Baafskathedraal, the
forbidding Geeraard de
Duivelsteen is a fortified palace
of splendid Romanesque
design built of grey limestone
in the thirteenth century. The
stronghold, bordered by what
remains of its moat, takes its
name from Geeraard Vilain,
who earned the soubriquet
"duivel" (devil) for his acts of
cruelty or, according to some
sources, because of his swarthy
features and black hair. Vilain
was not the only noble to wall
himself up within a castle – well
into the fourteenth century,
Ghent was dotted with fortified
houses (*stenen*), such was the
fear the privileged few had of
the rebellious guildsmen. The
last noble moved out of the
Duivelsteen in about
1350 and since then the
building has been put to a
bewildering range of uses – at
various times it served as an
arsenal, a prison, a madhouse
and an orphanage; nowadays it
houses government offices.

Lieven Bauwensplein and the van Eyck monument

Just south of the Duivelsteen is
Lieven Bauwensplein, a square
that takes its name from – and
has a statue of – the local
entrepreneur who founded the
city's machine-manufactured
textile industry. Born in 1769,
the son of a tanner, Bauwens
was an intrepid soul, who posed

▼ GEERAARD DE DUIVELSTEEM

Shops

▲ ALEPPO

Aleppo
Oudburg 70 ☏ 04 77 33 98 56, Mon noon–5.30pm, Tues–Sat noon–6.30pm. Designer secondhand clothes for men and women, including big names like Ralph Lauren and Armani. Specializes in (believe it or not) cowboy outfits, with an abundance of leather and denim. The first floor is dedicated to 1960s and 1970s retro gear.

as an ordinary textile worker in England to learn how its (much more technologically advanced) machinery worked. In the 1790s, he managed to smuggle a spinning jenny over to the continent and soon opened cotton mills in Ghent. It didn't, however, do Bauwens much good; he over-borrowed and when there was a downturn in demand, his factories went bust and he died in poverty.

North of the square, on Limburgstraat, stands a monument to the Eyck brothers, Hubert and Jan, the painter(s) of the *Adoration of the Mystic Lamb*. The monument is a somewhat stodgy affair, knocked up for the Great Exhibition of 1913, but it's an interesting piece of art propaganda, proclaiming Hubert as co-painter of the altarpiece, when this is very speculative (see p.111). Open on Hubert's knees is the Bible's Revelations, which may or may not have given him artistic inspiration.

Alternatief
Baudelostraat 15 ☏ 09 223 23 11. Mon–Sat 11am–6.30pm. Great range of good-quality secondhand clothes and paraphernalia. Take a moment to browse the shop at the back as well, where you'll find everything from old cars to the last in kitsch.

Bethsabis
Hoogpoort 5 ☏ 09 225 54 54. Mon–Fri 9.45am–noon & 12.45–6pm, Sat 9.45am–6pm. Bargain shoe shop offering big names at low prices – snap up a pair of Prada shoes, for example, at half the regular price.

Claudia Sträter
Kalandestraat 6 ☏ 09 233 78 40. Mon–Thurs 10am–6pm, Fri & Sat 10am–6.30pm. This Dutch designer has gained an international reputation amongst women in the last few years and is especially popular in Belgium. The shop's light and spacious interior offers

Central Ghent

the perfect setting for Sträter's stylish collections, which include feminine tailored jackets and quality sporty casuals.

Cora Kemperman
Mageleinstraat 38 ☎09 233 77 83, ⊛www.corakemperman.nl. Mon–Sat 10am–6pm. This much lauded Dutch designer is popular amongst Belgian women for her unique but accessible designs in natural colours and fabrics.

Count's Gallery
Rekelingestraat 1 ☎09 225 31 27. Wed–Sun 10am–6pm. This odd little shop, just opposite Het Gravensteen, sells an eclectic range of souvenirs, miniature models, postcards and so forth – great for kitsch gifts.

Dulce
Jan Breydelstraat 1 ☎09 223 48 73. Tues–Sat 10am–6pm. One of the best independent chocolate makers in Ghent – the handmade pralines are delectable.

The Fallen Angels
Jan Breydelstraat 29–31 ☎09 223 94 15, ⊛www.the-fallen-angels .com. Wed–Sat 1–6pm. Mother and daughter run these two adjacent shops, selling all manner of old bric-a-brac from postcards and posters through to teddy bears

▲ THE FALLEN ANGELS

and toys. Intriguing at best, twee at worst, but a useful source of unusual gifts.

Galerie St John
Bij St Jacobs 15 ☎09 225 82 62. Mon–Thurs 2–6pm, Fri & Sat 10am–noon & 2–6pm, Sun 10am–noon. One of several antique shops in the vicinity, this place sells an alluring range of objets d'art from silverware and chandeliers through to oil paintings. Great location, too – in an old church overlooking this busy square.

Interphilia
St Baafsplein 4 ☎09 225 46 80. Mon & Wed–Sat 10am–noon & 1–5.30pm. Temptingly old-fashioned stamp shop (with a sideline in coins), where every nook and cranny is stuffed to the gills.

Kloskanthuis
Jan Breydelstraat 2 ☎09 223 60 93. Tues–Sat 10am–6pm. Ghent's one and only specialist lace shop, though the lace is actually part of a wider line in home linen. Well presented and displayed, though Bruges has more choice – see p.77 & p.101.

Neuhaus
St Baafsplein 20 ☎09 223 43 74, ⊛www.neuhaus.be. Daily 10am–6pm. Belgium's best chocolate chain, with mouthwatering chocolates at €11 for 250g – try their Manons, stuffed white chocolates, which come with fresh cream, vanilla and coffee fillings.

Obius
Meerseniersstraat 4 ☎09 223 82 69, ⊛www.obius.be. Mon 1.30–6.30pm, Tues–Sat 10.30am–6.30pm. This friendly shoe and clothes shop, catering for both men and women, has all the designer

Markets

Ghent does a good line in open-air markets. There's a large and popular flea market (**prondelmarkt**) on Bij St Jacobs and adjoining Beverhoutplein (Fri, Sat & Sun 8am–1pm); a daily flower market on the Kouter, on the south side of the centre, just off Veldstraat (7am–1pm); organic foodstuffs on the Groentenmarkt (Fri 7.30am–1pm); and a bird market (not for the squeamish) on the Vrijdagmarkt on Sundays (7am–1pm).

gear you need, including Prada, Bruno Pieters, Miu-Miu and Patrick Cox, among many others.

Olivier Strelli (for men)

Stiletto, Volderstraat 19 ⓣ09 225 82 20, ⓦwww.strelli.be. Mon–Sat 10am–6pm. Showcases Strelli's stylish if pricey men's collection, including sharp, well-tailored suits and smart casual wear.

Olivier Strelli (for women)

Kalandestraat 19 ⓣ09 233 62 85, ⓦwww.strelli.be. Mon–Sat 10am–6pm. The main Ghent emporium of Olivier Strelli, arguably Belgium's leading designer, offering simple but chic modern clothes for women. Specializes in smart tailored skirts and dresses in zesty coloured fabrics. Expensive.

Peeters Delicatessen

Hoornstraat 9 ⓣ09 225 69 68. Mon–Sat 9am–6.30pm. Petite cheese and wine shop with a traditional feel to it, even down to the owner's apron and hat. Stocks an excellent range of Belgian cheeses, as well as a good selection of jam and marmalade.

Tierenteyn

Groetenmarkt 3. Mon–Sat 8.30am–6pm. This traditional shop, one of the city's most delightful, makes its own mustards – wonderful, tongue-tickling stuff displayed in shelf upon shelf of ceramic jars. A small jar will set you back about €6.

't Vlaams Wandtapijt

St Baafsplein 6 ⓣ09 223 16 43. Mon–Sat 9.30am–6pm. The great days of Belgian tapestry manufacture are long gone, but the industry survives, albeit in diminished form, and this shop features its products. The large tapestries on sale here are mostly richly decorated modern renditions of traditional motifs and styles. As you might expect, they're expensive (from around €500), though there's also a good range of much more affordable stuff like cushion covers, handbags and other smaller knick-knacks.

Cafés

Brooderie

Jan Breydelstraat 8. Tues–Sun 8am–6pm. Pleasant and informal café with a health-food slant, offering wholesome breakfasts, lunches, sandwiches and salads (from around €9), plus cakes and coffee. Also offers bed and breakfast (see p.150).

Patisserie Bloch

Veldstraat 60, on the corner with Voldersstraat. Mon, Tues & Thurs 9.30am–6pm, Fri & Sat 9.30am-5pm. Something of a local institution, and a favourite with shoppers for donkey's years, this tearoom offers a lip-smacking variety of cakes and confectioneries, washed down with premium coffees and teas. Snacks are available too – though these are no great shakes – and there's a takeaway service. The decor is really rather ordinary – the place is a bit like a canteen – but if you like cakes you won't give a hoot.

Souplounge

Zuivelbrug 4, just off Vrijdagmarkt. Daily 10am–7pm. Bright and cheerful modern café where the big bowls of freshly made soup are the main event – from €6. Self-service.

Restaurants

De 3 Biggetjes

Zeugsteeg 7 ☎09 224 46 48, ⓦwww.de3biggetjes.com. Mon, Tues, Thurs & Fri noon–2pm & 7–9pm, Sat 7–9pm, Sun noon–2pm. In the heart of the Patershol, this charmingly intimate restaurant occupies an old terrace house with a trim crowstep gable. A select but extremely well-chosen menu features the freshest of ingredients prepared with creative gusto – locally reared antelope in *jenever* sauce for example. Main courses from €20.

▼ BIJ DEN WIJZEN EN DEN ZOT

Amadeus

Plotersgracht 8 ☎09 225 13 85. Mon–Wed 7–11pm, Thurs noon–2.30pm & 7–11pm, Fri–Sun noon–2.30pm & 6pm–midnight. In the heart of the Patershol, this busy, well-established restaurant specializes in spare ribs. Long tables, oodles of stained glass, low ceilings and an eccentric sprinkling of bygones makes the place relaxed and convivial. Main courses at around €20.

Avalon

Geldmunt 32 ☎09 224 37 24. Mon–Thurs 11.30am–2.30pm, Fri & Sat 11.30am–2.30pm & 6–9pm. This spick-and-span vegetarian restaurant offers a wide range of well-prepared food. The key pull is the daily lunchtime specials, which cost about €9. Choose from one of the many different rooms inside or the terrace at the back in the summer.

Bij den wijzen en den zot

Hertogstraat 42 ☎09 223 42 30. Tues–Sat noon–2pm & 6.30–9.30pm. One of the better restaurants in the Patershol, serving up Flemish cuisine with more than a dash of French flair. Soft lighting and classical music set the tone. The premises are charming too – an old brick house of tiny rooms and narrow stairs with dining on two floors. Prices are bearable, with main courses averaging

House of Eliott

Jan Breydelstraat 36 ℗09 225 21 28,
ⓦwww.thehouseofeliott.be.
Mon & Thurs–Sun noon–2pm &
6–10pm. Idiosyncratic, spilt-
level restaurant strewn with
Edwardian bric-a-brac and
offering a limited but well-
chosen menu of meat and fish
dishes, all freshly prepared and
very tasty. The window tables
overlook a canal and, if the
weather holds, you can eat out
on the pontoon at the back.
Mains €20–25.

Malatesta

Korenmarkt 35. Daily except Tues
11.30am–2.30pm & 6–11pm.
Informally fashionable café-
restaurant decorated in strong,
modern style and offering tasty
pizza and pasta dishes from €12.
Handy location too, bang in the
centre of the city.

Marco Polo Trattoria

Serpentstraat 11 ℗09 225 04 20.
Tues–Fri noon–2.30pm & 6–10pm,
Sat & Sun 6–10pm. This simple
rustic restaurant is part of the
Italian "slow food" movement
in which the emphasis is on
organic, seasonal ingredients
prepared in a traditional
manner. The menu is small,
but all the dishes are freshly
prepared and delicious. Mains
from €13.

▲ DE BLAUWE ZALM

about €24; house specialities
include eel, cooked in several
different ways, and *waterzooi*
(fish or chicken stew).

De Blauwe Zalm

Vrouwebroersstraat 2 ℗09 224
08 52. Mon & Sat 7–9.30pm,
Tues–Fri noon–2pm & 7–9.30pm.
Outstanding seafood restaurant
– the best in town – serving
up everything from the more
usual cod, salmon, monkfish
and haddock though to the
likes of seawolf, sea bass, turbot
and John Dory. Fish tanks keep
the crustacea alive and kicking,
and the decor has a distinctly
maritime feel – though it's all
done in impeccable, ultra-cool
style. Main courses from €20.
Reservations pretty
much essential.

Domestica

Onderbergen 27 ℗09 223 53 00.
Mon 6.30–10.30pm, Tues–Fri
noon–2.30pm & 6.30–10.30pm, Sat
6.30–10.30pm. Smart and chic
brasserie-restaurant serving up
an excellent range of Belgian
dishes – both French and
Flemish – in nouvelle cuisine
style. Has a garden terrace for
good-weather eating. Main
courses from €20.

▲ 'T DREUPELKOT

▲ DULLE GRIET

Pakhuis

Schuurkenstraat 4 (down a narrow alley near St Michielsbrug) ☎09 223 55 55, ⓦwww.pakhuis.be. Mon–Sat noon–2.30pm & 6.30–11pm. Set in an intelligently remodelled old warehouse with acres of glass and metal, this lively bistro-brasserie is one of Ghent's more fashionable restaurants, attracting a wide-ranging clientele. The extensive menu features Flemish and French cuisine, with mains averaging €18. There's a bar area too (Mon–Sat 11.30am–1am).

▲ ROCOCO

Bars and clubs

't Dreupelkot

Groentenmarkt 12. Daily: July & Aug from 6pm until late; Sept–June from 4pm until late. Cosy bar specializing in *jenever* (Dutch gin), of which it stocks more than 215 brands, all kept at icy temperatures – the vanilla flavour is particularly delicious. It's down a little alley leading off the Groentenmarkt – and next door to *Het Waterhuis*.

Dulle Griet

Vrijdagmarkt 50. Mon 4.30pm–1am, Tues–Sat noon–1am, Sun noon–7.30pm. Long, dark and atmospheric bar with all manner of incidental objets d'art and an especially wide range of beers.

Pink Flamingos

Onderstraat 55 ☎09 233 47 18, ⓦwww.pinkflamingos.be. Mon–Wed noon–midnight, Thurs & Fri noon–3am, Sat 2pm–3am, Sun 2pm–midnight. Weird and wonderful place, whose interior is the height of kitsch, with plastic statues of film stars, tacky religious icons and Barbie-dolls – if it's cheesy, you'll find it somewhere amidst and amongst the clutter. Attracts a groovy crowd, and is

---

a great place for an aperitif or cocktail.

Rococo

Corduwaniersstraat 57. Daily except Mon 10pm until late. This intimate café-cum-bar attracts a diverse but ultra-cool clientele and is a perfect place to be on a cold winter evening, with candles flickering and the fire roaring. Stocks a good range of wines and beers, and also has home-made cakes.

De Tempelier

Meersenierstraat 9. Wed–Sat 10pm until late. Few tourists venture into this small, dark and intriguing old bar, which offers a vast range of beers at lower-than-usual prices. The place attracts a sometimes eccentric clientele, plus frequent live bands. It's very close to Dulle Griet, off Vrijdagmarkt.

De Trollekelder

Bij St Jacobs 17. Mon–Thurs 5pm–2am & Fri–Sun 4pm–2am. This dark and atmospheric bar offers a huge selection of beers in an ancient merchant's house – don't be deterred by the trolls stuck in the window.

▲ DEN TURK

Den Turk

Botermarkt 3. Daily from 11am until late. The oldest bar in the city, this tiny rabbit-warren of a place offers a good range of beers and whiskies, but much of its atmosphere disappeared when it was recently renovated. Hosts frequent live music acts, mainly jazz.

Het Waterhuisaan de Bierkant

Groentenmarkt 9. Daily 11am until late. More than a hundred types of beer are available in this engaging, canalside bar, which is popular with tourists and locals alike. Be sure to try Stropken (literally "noose"), a delicious local brew named after the time in 1453 when Philip the Good compelled the rebellious city burghers to parade outside the town gate with ropes around their necks.

Southern and eastern Ghent

Although the majority of Ghent's key attractions are within easy strolling distance of the Korenmarkt, two of the city's principal museums are located some 2km south of the centre. These are the newly refurbished Museum voor Schone Kunsten (Fine Art Museum) and the adjacent Museum of Contemporary Art, S.M.A.K. Many visitors just hop on a tram at the Korenmarkt for the quick trip down to the two, but with a little more time the twenty-minute walk there can take in several less well-known sights. The route suggested below begins by heading south from the Korenmarkt along Veldstraat, Ghent's main shopping street, before dropping by the two museums.

East of St Baafskathedraal, Ghent's eighteenth- and nineteenth-century suburbs stretch out toward the Dampoort train station. Few tourists venture this way, which is hardly surprising given that the main attraction, the enchanting ruins of St Baafsabdij (St Bavo's Abbey), are currently closed, though you might check with the tourist office (see p.155) to see if they've been reopened.

St Baafsabdij

Spanjaardstraat. Closed until further notice. Beginning at the Duivelsteen (see p.122), the best route out to St Baafsabdij is along Reep and then Gebroeders Van Eyckstraat. The latter leads to the bridge over the River Leie, on the far side of which turn left and first right down Spanjaardstraat. The extensive ruins of St Baafsabdij ramble over a narrow parcel of land beside the river, occupying what was once a strategically important location. It was here, in 630, that the French missionary St Amand founded an abbey, though the locals could not have been overly impressed as they ended up drowning him in the river. Nonetheless, St Amand's abbey survived to become a famous place of pilgrimage on account of its guardianship of the remains of the seventh-century St Bavo. In the ninth century, the abbey suffered a major disaster when the Vikings decided this was the ideal spot to camp while they raided the surrounding region, but order was eventually restored, another colony of monks moved in and the abbey was rebuilt in 950. The Emperor Charles V had most of this second abbey knocked down in the 1540s and the monks decamped to St Baafskathedraal, but somehow the ruins managed to survive.

If the abbey is closed, as is presently the case, the only thing you'll see is the retaining wall, but inside the abbey's extensive ruins include the remnants of an ivy-covered Gothic cloister, whose long vaulted corridors are attached to a distinctive, octagonal tower, comprising a toilet on the bottom floor and the storage room – the sanctuarium – for the St Bavo relic up above. The lower level of the substantial two-storey building attached to the cloister holds all sorts of architectural bits and pieces retrieved from the city during renovations and demolitions. There are gargoyles and finely carved Gothic heads, terracotta panels, broken off chunks of columns and capitals, and several delightful mini-tableaux. There's precious little labelling, but it's the skill of the carving that impresses and, if you've already explored the city, one or two pieces are identifiable, principally the original lion from the old punishment post on St Veerleplein (see p.119). A flight of steps leads up from beside the museum to the Romanesque refectory, a splendid chamber whose magnificent, hooped timber roof dates – remarkably enough – from the twelfth century. The grounds of the abbey are small, but they are partly wild, a flurry of shrubs and flowers that are absolutely delightful – and perfect for a picnic.

Veldstraat

The city's main shopping street, Veldstraat, leads south from the Korenmarkt, running parallel to the River Leie. By and large, it's a very ordinary strip, but the eighteenth-century mansion at no.82 hold the modest Museum Arnold Vander Haeghen (Mon–Fri 9am–noon & 2–5pm; free), where pride of place goes to the Chinese salon, whose original silk wallpaper has survived intact. The Duke of Wellington stayed here in 1815 after the Battle of Waterloo, popping across the street to the Hôtel d'Hane-Steenhuyse, at no.55, to bolster the morale of the refugee King of France, Louis XVIII (see box, p.134). Dating to 1768, the grand facade of Louis's hideaway has survived in good condition, its elaborate pediment sporting allegorical representations of Time and History, but at present there's no access to the expansive salons beyond.

Pushing on down Veldstraat, it's a couple of minutes further to a matching pair of grand, Neoclassical nineteenth-century buildings. On the right hand side is the Justitiepaleis (Palace of Justice), whose colossal pediment sports a frieze with the figure of Justice in the middle, the accused to one side and the condemned on the other. Opposite stands the grandiloquent opera house, home to De Vlaamse Opera (see p.158) – its facade awash with playfully decorative stone panels.

From the opera house, it's an easy, if dull, ten-minute stroll south to S.M.A.K. and the Museum voor Schone Kunsten via the Nederkouter,

▲ PALACE OF JUSTICE

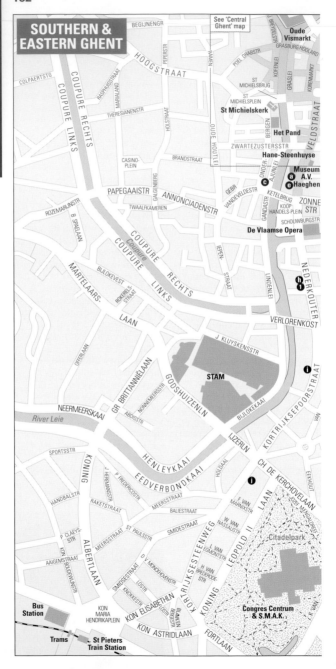

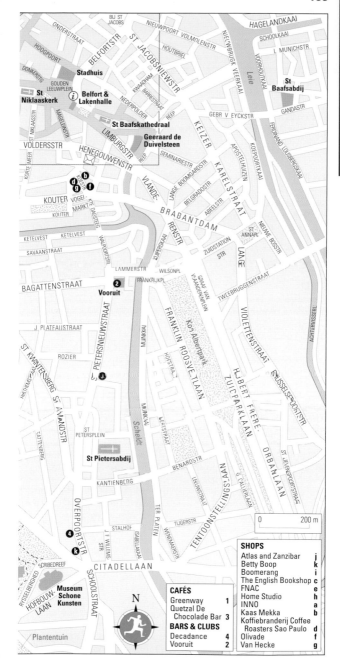

CAFÉS
Greenway 1
Quetzal De
Chocolade Bar 3

BARS & CLUBS
Decadance 4
Vooruit 2

SHOPS
Atlas and Zanzibar j
Betty Boop k
Boomerang i
The English Bookshop c
FNAC e
Home Studio h
INNO a
Kaas Mekka b
Koffiebranderij Coffee
Roasters Sao Paulo d
Olivade f
Van Hecke g

Louis XVIII in Ghent

Abandoning his throne, Louis had hot-footed it to Ghent soon after Napoleon landed in France following his escape from Elba. While others did his fighting for him, Louis waited around in Ghent gorging himself – his daily dinner lasted all of seven hours and the bloated exile was known to polish off one hundred oysters at a sitting. His fellow exile, the writer and politician François Chateaubriand, ignored the gluttony and cowardice, writing meekly that "The French alone know how to dine with method". Thanks to Wellington's ministrations, Louis was persuaded to return to his kingdom and his entourage left for Paris on June 26, 1815, one week after Waterloo.

but it's better – and not much longer – to walk along the banks of the River Leie: turn off Nederkouter at Verlorenkost and then – with the Coupure canal and its dinky swing bridge dead ahead – hang a left along the river.

STAM

Godshuizenlaan. Founded in the thirteenth century, the old Cistercian Bijlokeabdij (Bijloke Abbey) on Godshuizenlaan, just to the west of the River Leie, was savaged by Calvinists on several occasions, but much of the medieval complex has survived, its tidy brown-brick buildings set behind a handsome Baroque portal. The abbey is currently closed to visitors as part of a major redevelopment which will create STAM (www.stamgent.be), a museum devoted to the city's heritage. The surrounding grounds are being redeveloped too with the creation of a concert hall, studios and an academy. The work is scheduled for completion in 2009.

Citadelpark

Open access; free. Citadelpark takes its name from the fortress that stood here until the 1870s, when the land was cleared and prettified with a network of leafy footpaths steering

their way past grottoes and ponds, statues and fountains, a waterfall and a bandstand. These nineteenth-century niceties survive today and this is what you still see in good order, though a large brick complex was added on the east side of the park in the 1940s which is now occupied by a conference centre and S.M.A.K (see below). If you've spent a lot of time in Flanders, however, Citadelpark is remarkable for one thing: a hill – just about everywhere else is pancake flat.

S.M.A.K.

Citadelpark. Tues–Sun 10am–6pm; €5; www.smak.be. One of Belgium's most adventurous contemporary art galleries, S.M.A.K. (the Stedelijk Museum voor Actuele Kunst, or Municipal Museum of Contemporary Art) is given over to temporary exhibitions of international quality supplemented by a regularly rotated selection of sculptures, paintings and installations distilled from the museum's wide-ranging permanent collection. S.M.A.K. possesses examples of all the major artistic movements since World War II – everything from surrealism, the CoBrA group and pop art through to minimalism and conceptual art, as well as their forerunners, most notably René Magritte and Paul Delvaux. Perennial favourites include the installations of the influential German Joseph Beuys (1921–86), who played a leading role in the European avant-garde art movement of the 1970s, and a characteristically unnerving painting by Francis Bacon (1909–92) entitled *A Figure Sitting*.

Museum voor Schone Kunsten (Fine Art Museum)

Citadelpark. Tues–Sun 10am–6pm; €4; ⊛www.mskgent.be. Directly opposite S.M.A.K. is Ghent's largest and most acclaimed art gallery, the recently refurbished Museum voor Schone Kunsten, which occupies an imposing Neoclassical edifice on the eastern edge of Citadelpark. Inside, the central atrium and connecting rotunda are flanked by a sequence of rooms, with older paintings exhibited to the right in Rooms 1–8, the bulk of the eighteenth- and nineteenth-century collection in Rooms 13–19, and early twentieth-century works mostly on the left in Rooms A–S. There's not enough space to display all the permanent collection at any one time, so there's some rotation, but you can expect to see the paintings mentioned below even if they aren't in the

room described. The layout of the collection doesn't seem to follow much of a scheme, but it's small enough to be easily manageable; free museum plans are issued at reception.

Beginning with the numbered rooms on the right, one highlight of the museum's small but eclectic collection of early Flemish paintings is Rogier van der Weyden's (1399–1464) *Madonna with Carnation*, the proffered flower serving as a symbol of Christ's passion. Also in Room 2 are two works by Hieronymus Bosch (1450–1516), most notably his *Bearing of the Cross*, showing Christ mocked by some of the most grotesque and deformed characters Bosch ever painted. Look carefully and you'll see that Christ's head is at the centre of two diagonals, one representing evil, the other good – the latter linking the repentant thief with St Veronica, whose cloak carries the imprint of Christ's face. Moving on, highlights include *Mary and Child* by Adriaen Isenbrandt (d.1551) in Room 3; a powerful *St Francis* by Rubens (1577–1640) in Room 5; and the robust romanticism of the *Judgement of Midas* by Jacob Jordaens (1593–1678) in Room 7. Jordaens was greatly influenced by Rubens, but was also capable of much greater

▼ S.M.A.K.

subtlety – his *Studies of the Head of Abraham Grapheus*, also in Room 7, is an example of the high-quality preparatory paintings he completed, most of which were later recycled within larger compositions. In the same room, Anthony van Dyck's (1599–1641) *Jupiter and Antiope* wins the bad taste award for its portrayal of the lecherous god, with his tongue hanging out in anticipation of sex with Antiope.

Room P displays one of the museum's most celebrated paintings, the *Self-Portrait with Flower Hat* by James Ensor (1860–1949), whose remarkable work can also be seen in Rooms F, I, J and K. Room R is distinguished by two harrowing studies by Ostend's Leon Spilliaert (1881–1946), while Room C displays several characteristically unsettling works by Paul Delvaux (1897–1994) and René Magritte (1898–1967), most memorably the latter's *Persepective II. Manet's Balcony*, in which the figures from Manet's painting have been replaced by wooden coffins.

Overpoortstraat and St Pietersabdij

From just to the east of the Fine Art Museum, Overpoortstraat runs north through the heart of the city's student quarter, a gritty and grimy but vivacious district, jam-packed with late-night bars and inexpensive cafés. Overpoortstraat finally emerges on St Pietersplein, a very wide and very long cobbled square flanked by the sprawling mass of **St Pietersabdij** (St Peter's Abbey). The abbey dates back to the earliest days of the city and was probably founded by St Amand in about 640. The Vikings razed the original buildings three centuries later, but it was rebuilt on a grand scale and became rich and powerful in equal measure. In 1578, the Protestants destroyed the abbey as a symbol of much that they hated and the present complex – a real Baroque monstrosity incorporating two courtyard complexes – was erected in the seventeenth and eighteenth centuries. The last monks were ejected during the French occupation in 1796 and since then – as with many other ecclesiastical complexes in Belgium – it's been hard to figure out any suitable use. Today, much of the complex serves as municipal offices, but visitors can pop into the domed St Pieterskerk, which was modelled on St Peter's in Rome, though the interior is no more than a plodding Baroque.

To the right of the church, part of the old monastic complex has been turned into an arts exhibition centre, the **Kunsthal St Pietersabdij** (Tues–Sun 10am–6pm; free, though some exhibitions charge an entrance fee). Several of the adjacent cellars, rooms and corridors can also be explored with "Alison", a multilingual audioguide geared up for teens and pre-teens (same times; €6). There's precious little to actually see here, but youngsters seem to enjoy this miniature labyrinth.

Vooruit

St Pietersnieuwstraat 23 ☏ 09 267 28 28, ⊛ www.vooruit.be. Café-bar: Mon–Thurs 11.30am–2am, Fri & Sat 11.30am–3am, Sun 4pm–2am. It's a brief stroll north from St Pietersplein to Vooruit, a café-cum-performing arts centre that is, to all intents and purposes, the cultural heart of the city (at least for the under-40s), offering a varied programme of rock and pop through to dance. Vooruit also occupies a splendid building, a twin-towered and turreted former Festival Hall that was built for Ghent's socialists in an eclectic rendition of Art Nouveau in 1914.

Shops

Atlas and Zanzibar

Kortrijksesteenweg 19 ⓣ 09 220 87 99, ⓦ www.atlaszanzibar.be. Mon–Fri 10am–1pm & 2–6.30pm, Sat 10am–1pm & 2–6pm. Specialist travel bookshop offering a comprehensive selection of Belgian hiking maps and many English guidebooks.

Betty Boop

Overpoortstraat 110 ⓣ 09 222 05 76, ⓦ www.bettyboop.be. Mon, Tues, Thurs & Fri noon–7pm, Wed 2–7pm & Sat noon–6pm. All the best Belgian comics, both traditional and new, plus a selection from America and manga from Japan.

Boomerang

Kortrijksepoortstraat 142 ⓣ 09 225 37 07 Tues–Sat 2–6.15pm. One of the best and most stylish retro and secondhand clothing shops in the city; also has a good

selection of shoes for men and women.

The English Bookshop

Ajuinlei 15 ⓣ 09 223 02 36. Mon–Sat 10am–6pm. Small, but well-stocked secondhand bookstore selling all sorts of cheap English-language books, particularly on historical and military subjects.

FNAC

Veldstraat 88 ⓣ 09 223 40 80, ⓦ www .fnac.be. Mon–Sat 10am–6.30pm. Several floors of music, books and newspapers, including a good English-language section. It's also excellent for maps, including a comprehensive range of Belgian hiking maps, and sells tickets for most mainstream cultural events.

Home Studio

Nederkouter 30 ⓣ 0473 93 05 72. Wed, Fri & Sat 10am–6pm. Specialists in chic Italian contemporary furniture. Very minimalist, and all in neutral tones.

INNO

Veldstraat 86 ⓣ 09 225 58 65 Mon–Thurs & Sat 9.30am–6pm, Fri 9.30am–7pm. This large Belgian department store specializes in clothes, and also has a good

▼ BOSCH PAINTING, ST BAAFSKATHEDRAAL

games and toys department, plus household goods.

Kaas Mekka

Koestraat 9 ☎09 225 83 66. Tues–Sat 8am–6.30pm. Literally the "Cheese Mecca", this small specialist cheese shop offers a remarkable range of traditional and exotic cheeses – try some of the delicious Ghent goats' cheese (*geitenkaas*).

Koffiebranderij Coffee Roasters Sao Paulo

Koestraat 24 ☎09 225 44 11. Mon 12.30–6.30pm, Tues–Sat 9am–6.30pm. Excellent range of coffee, either pre-packed or freshly ground to your specifications, plus all sorts of other coffee paraphernalia.

Olivade

Koestraat 25 ☎09 225 40 42. Tues–Sat 10am–6pm. Gift shop-cum-foodstore specializing in all things to do with olives, from the stuffed variety (free tastings available) to oils, vinegar and marinades. Also has a small selection of takeaway pasta and rolls.

Van Hecke

Koestraat 42 ☎09 225 43 57. Mon–Sat except Wed 9.30am–6pm. Independent chocolatier, arguably the best in town, selling handmade chocolates rustled up on the premises. Sells cakes too.

Cafés

Greenway

Nederkouter 42. Mon-Sat 11am-9pm. Straightforward café-cum-takeaway decorated in sharp modern style, selling a wide range of "green" foods, from bio-burgers to pastas, noodles and baguettes, all for just a few euros.

Quetzal De Chocolade Bar

St-Pietersnieuwstraat 99. Mon–Thurs 7am–11pm, Fri–Sun 1–7pm, July & Aug daily 1–7pm only. Chocolate aficionados will get their fix in this bright and modern café devoted to the cocoa bean. Treats on offer range from the humble chocolate chip cookie to a chocolate fondue for two, as well as a plethora of chocolate-flavoured drinks, and coffee. Takeaway available.

Bars and clubs

Decadance

Overpoortstraat 76 ☎09 329 00 54. Daily from 10pm until 8–10am, Sun until midnight. This funky/grungy club near the university (hence the abundance of students) offers one of the city's best nights out, with reggae, hip-hop, drum 'n' bass and garage-techno vibes.

Vooruit

St Pietersnieuwstraat 23 ☎09 267 28 28, ⓦ www.vooruit.be. Café-bar: Mon–Thurs 11.30am–2am, Fri & Sat 11.30am–3am, Sun 4pm–2am. The Vooruit performing arts centre has good claim to be the city's cultural centre (at least for under-40s), offering a wide-ranging programme of rock and pop through to dance. (It also occupies a splendid building, a twin-towered and turreted former hall that was built for Ghent's socialists in an eclectic rendition of Art Nouveau in 1914.) The café-bar is a large barn-like affair that gets jam-packed till well into the morning.

Accommodation

Accommodation

The great thing about staying in either Bruges or Ghent is that most of the more interesting and enjoyable hotels are in or near the centre, which is exactly where you want to be. The main difference is that in Bruges you're spoilt for choice as the city has scores of hotels, whereas Ghent has a more limited – if just as select – range.

Bruges

Bruges has over one hundred hotels, dozens of bed-and-breakfasts and several unofficial youth hostels, but still can't accommodate all its visitors at the height of the season. If you're arriving in July or August, be sure to book ahead or, at a pinch, make sure you get here in the morning before all the rooms have gone. Given the crush, many visitors use the efficient hotel and B&B **booking service** provided by the the main tourist office in the Concertgebouw (see p.155) – bookings can be made both on the spot and in advance via their website (®www.brugge .be). At other times of the year, things are usually much less pressing, though it's still a good idea to reserve ahead especially if you're picky – it's easy enough, as almost everyone in the accommodation business speaks (at least some) English. Standards are generally high, but note that hoteliers are wont to deck out their foyers rather grandly, often in contrast to the spartan rooms beyond, while many places offer rooms of widely divergent size and comfort. We've reviewed twenty of the best places below; in addition, the city's tourist office issues a free accommodation booklet providing comprehensive listings.

The **centre** is liberally sprinkled with hotels, many of which occupy quaint and/or elegant old buildings. There's a cluster immediately to the south of one of the two main squares, the Burg – though places here tend to be expensive – and another, more affordable group in the vicinity of the Spiegelrei canal, one of the prettiest and quieter parts of the centre. Most of the city's hotels are small – twenty rooms, often less – and few are owned by a chain. Almost all hotels offer **breakfast** at no extra (or minimal) charge, ranging from a roll and coffee at the less expensive places through to full-scale banquets at the top end of the range. Finally, note that the hotel room prices given below do not take into account special or weekend discounts.

B&Bs are generously distributed across the city centre too, and many offer excellent

---

Hotel stars and prices

All licensed Belgian hotels carry a blue permit shield indicating the number of stars allocated (up to a maximum of five). This classification system is, by necessity, measured against easily identifiable criteria – toilets, room service, lifts, and so on – rather than aesthetics or specific location, and consequently can only provide a general guide to quality and prices.

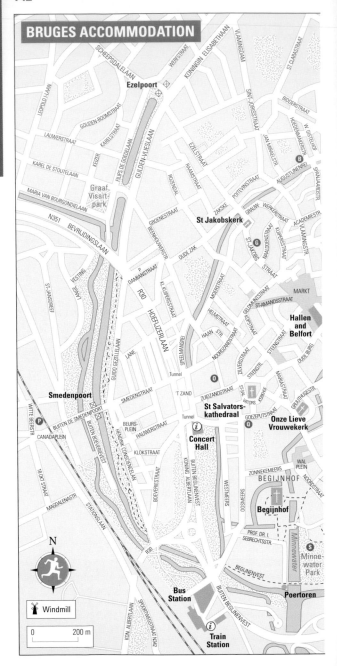

BRUGES ACCOMMODATION

Ezelpoort

St Jakobskerk

Hallen and Belfort

MARKT

Smedenpoort

'T ZAND

St Salvators-kathedraal

Onze Lieve Vrouwekerk

Concert Hall

BEGIJNHOF

Begijnhof

Minnewater Park

Poertoren

Bus Station

Train Station

N

🪂 Windmill

0   200 m

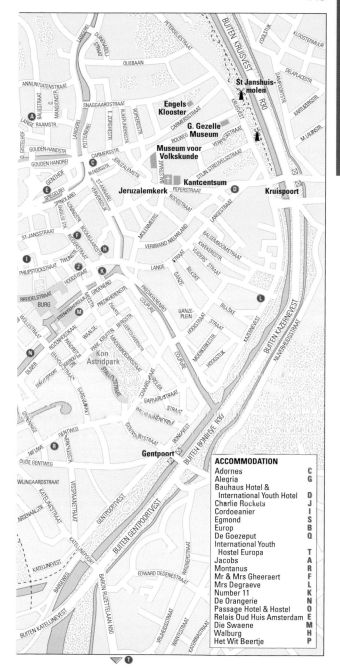

ACCOMMODATION

Adornes	C
Alegria	G
Bauhaus Hotel & International Youth Hotel	D
Charlie Rockets	J
Cordoeanier	I
Egmond	S
Europ	B
De Goezeput	Q
International Youth Hostel Europa	T
Jacobs	A
Montanus	R
Mr & Mrs Gheeraert	F
Mrs Degraeve	L
Number 11	K
De Orangerie	N
Passage Hotel & Hostel	O
Relais Oud Huis Amsterdam	E
Die Swaene	M
Walburg	H
Het Wit Beertje	P

en-suite accommodation for around €60–70 per double, although some of the more luxurious establishments charge in the region of €90–100. In addition, Bruges has a handful of unofficial **youth hostels**, offering dormitory beds at around €16 per person per night. Most of these places, as well as the official HI youth hostel, which is tucked away in the suburbs, also have a limited supply of smaller rooms, with doubles for about €35–45 per night.

Hotels

Adornes St Annarei 26 ☎050 34 13 36, ⓦ www.adornes.be. Three-star hotel in a tastefully converted old Flemish town house, with a plain, high-gabled facade. Both the public areas and the comfortable bedrooms are decorated in bright whites and creams, which emphasizes the antique charm of the place. It enjoys an excellent location, too, at the junction of two canals near the east end of Spiegelrei, and delicious breakfasts. Also very child-friendly – high chairs for the dining room are, for example, no problem. Doubles €100–130.

Alegria Sint Jakobsstraat 34 ☎050 33 09 37, ⓦ www.alegria-hotel.com. This appealing, family-run three-star has just six well-appointed rooms, each decorated in pastel greens, creams and whites. The rooms at the back, overlooking the garden are quieter than those at the front. Great location too – a brief stroll from the Markt. Doubles €80–120.

Bauhaus Budget Hotel Langestraat 133 ☎050 34 10 93, ⓦ www.bauhaus.be. Next to the *Bauhaus Hostel* (see p.146), this one-star hotel offers 21 very spartan rooms with shower and basin. Very popular with backpackers thanks to its cheap singles, doubles, triples and quads, but don't expect too much in the way of creature comforts, and the rooms are a little dingy. Laidback, occasionally boisterous atmosphere plus a (usually) friendly clientele. Doubles €50. €40–50

Cordoeanier Cordoeaniersstraat 18 ☎050 33 90 51, ⓦ www.cordoeanier.be. Medium-sized, family-run two-star handily

located in a narrow side-street a couple of minutes' walk north of the Burg. Mosquitoes can be a problem, but the small rooms are clean and pleasant. Doubles €70–95.

Egmond Minnewater 15 ☎050 34 14 45, ⓦ www.egmond.be. Set in an old manor house, this rambling three star stands in a quiet location in its own gardens just metres from the Minnewater. The interior has wooden beamed ceilings and fine eighteenth-century chimneypieces, while the eight guest rooms are comfortable and surprisingly affordable. Doubles €90–140.

Europ Augustijnenrei 18 ☎050 33 79 75, ⓦ www.hoteleurop.com. Two-star hotel in a dignified late nineteenth-century town house overlooking a canal about five minutes' walk north of the Burg. It's a pleasant place to stay, even if the public areas are frumpy and some of the modern bedrooms a tad spartan. Doubles €60–130.

De Goezeput Goezeputstraat 29 ☎050 34 26 94, ⓦ www.hotelgoezeput.be. Set in a charming location on a quiet street near the cathedral, this outstanding two-star hotel occupies an immaculately refurbished eighteenth-century convent complete with wooden beams and oodles of antiques. A snip, with en-suite doubles for €75–95.

Jacobs Baliestraat 1 ☎050 33 98 31, ⓦ www.hoteljacobs.be. Pleasant three-star set in a creatively modernized old brick building complete with a precipitous crow-step gable. The twenty-odd rooms are decorated in brisk modern style, though some are a little small. It's in a quiet location in an attractive part of the centre, a ten-minute walk northeast of the Markt. Doubles €60–80.

Montanus Nieuwe Gentweg 78 ☎050 33 11 76, ⓦ www.montanus.be. Smart four-star hotel occupying a substantial seventeenth-century mansion kitted out in crisp modern style – although most of the rooms are at the back, in chalet-like accommodation at the far end of a large and attractive garden. There's also an especially appealing room in what amounts to a (cosy and luxurious) garden shed. Doubles €110–200.

De Orangerie Kartuizerinnenstraat 10 ☎050 34 16 49, ⓦ www.hotelorangerie .com. Excellent four-star hotel in a surprisingly quiet location a couple of minutes south of the Burg. The original eighteenth-century mansion has been remodelled and extended in opulent style to house twenty elegant bedrooms – though some are quite small – and there's a charming terrace bar at the back overlooking the canal. Doubles €150–275.

Passage Hotel Dweersstraat 28 ☎050 34 02 32, ⓦwww.passagebruges.com. A ten-minute stroll west of the Markt, this hotel is a real steal, with simple but well-maintained en-suite doubles for just €60, plus doubles with shared facilities from €45. It's a very popular spot and there are only ten rooms (four en suite) so advance reservations are pretty much essential. The busy bar serves inexpensive meals and is a favourite with backpackers. The inexpensive *Passage Hostel* (see p.146) is next door. Doubles €45–60.

Relais Oud Huis Amsterdam Spiegelrei 3 ☎050 34 18 10, ⓦwww .oha.be. Smooth, tastefully turned-out four-star hotel in a grand eighteenth-century mansion overlooking the Spiegelrei canal. Many of the furnishings and fittings are period, but more so in the public areas than in the thirty-odd rooms. Doubles €150–250.

Die Swaene Steenhouwersdijk 1 ☎050 34 27 98, ⓦwww.dieswaene.com. The unassuming brick exterior of this long-established four-star hotel is deceptive, as each of the large rooms beyond is luxuriously furnished in an individual antique style, while the new annexe across the canal has ten sumptuously decorated suites complete with marble bathooms and lavish furnishings. The location is perfect too, beside a particularly pretty and peaceful section of canal a short walk from the Burg – which partly accounts for its reputation as one of the city's most "romantic" hotels. There's also a heated pool and sauna, and the breakfast will set you up for the best part of a day. Doubles €195–235.

Walburg Boomgaardstraat 13 ☎050 34 94 14, ⓦwww.hotelwalburg.be. Engaging four-star in an elegant nineteenth-century mansion – with splendidly large doors – a short walk east of the Burg along Hoogstraat. The rooms are smart and comfortable, and there are also capacious suites. Doubles €125–175.

Bed & breakfasts

Mr & Mrs Gheeraert Riddersstraat 9 ☎050 33 56 27, ⓦwww.bb-bruges.be.

Holiday apartments

There are plenty of holiday apartments in Bruges available for both long and short-term rental, and the best offer good value in attractive surroundings. The comprehensive accommodation brochure issued by the city's tourist office details over fifty of them, with prices ranging from as little as €350 per week for two people (€425 for four) up to around €500 (€650). The tourist office does not, however, arrange holiday apartment lettings – these must be arranged direct with the lessor. As ever, advance booking is strongly advised. The following are two particularly good options.

Peerdenstraat 16 (Mr and Mrs Dieltiens ☎050 33 42 94, ⓦwww .bedandbreakfastbruges.be). Centrally located apartment in the Huyze de Blockfluyt, at Peerdenstraat 16, comprising a two-storey flat that sleeps up to four people, with wooden floors, exposed beams and a kitchen; it also has an additional attic bed above the main double complete with its own dinky little ladder. From €385–455 per week for two.

Ridderspoor (Riddersstraat 18, ☎050 34 90 11, ⓦwww.ridderspoor.be). An immaculate apartment and two studios in the Ridderspoor, a beautiful nineteenth-century house. The ground-floor studio has a private terrace, while the top-floor open-plan apartment offers a (limited) view of the Burg. Both have their own kitchen. Studio prices are from €420–490 per week for two. There's often a minimum three-night stay.

The three en-suite guest rooms here are bright and smart, and occupy the top floor of a creatively modernized old house a short walk east from the Burg. No credit cards. Closed Jan. Doubles €60–65.

Mrs Degraeve Kazernevest 32 ☎050 34 57 11, ⊛www.bedandbreakfast marjandegraeve.be. Relaxed, friendly B&B with two eclectically decorated (read wacky) guest rooms with shared facilities. The place prides itself on its individuality – there's a musical toilet and the landlady brews her own bottled beer. Situated on the eastern edge of town, not far from the Kruispoort – which means that you miss the tourist droves, but that it's also a fair old hike to the Markt (although you can hire bikes here). No credit cards. Doubles €50.

Number 11 Peerdenstraat 11 ☎050 33 06 75, ⊛www.number11.be. In the heart of Bruges, on a traffic-free street, this first-rate B&B, with just two guest rooms and a suite, is a lavish affair, adorned with art and antiques in equal proportions – every comfort, and smashing breakfasts too. Doubles €125–145, suite €215.

Het Wit Beertje Witte Beerstraat 4 ☎050 45 08 88, ⊛www.hetwitbeertje .be. This modest little guesthouse-cum-B&B, with just three en-suite rooms, is a particularly good deal. It's located just west of the city centre, off Canadaplein, beyond the Smedenpoort. Doubles €45–55.

Hostels

Bauhaus International Youth Hotel Langestraat 135 ☎050 34 10 93, ⊛www.bauhaus.be. Laid-back hostel with few discernible rules, several large dormitories (sleeping up to eight people) and a mish-mash of double (€36) and triple rooms (€51). Not for the fastidious – the place is far from neat and trim, but there's bike rental, currency exchange and lockers, and the popular downstairs bar serves filling meals. The hostel is situated about fifteen minutes' walk east of the Burg, next to the bargain-basement *Bauhaus Hotel* (see p.144). From €14 per person for a dorm bed.

Charlie Rockets Hoogstraat 19 ☎050 33 06 60, ⊛www.charlierockets.com. The rooms in this busy hostel may not be as pristine as they were when it opened a few years ago, but it steals a march on its rivals by being so much closer to the Markt. Accommodation is either in dorms (sleeping four or six) or double rooms. It's above an American-style bar, so light sleepers may prefer to go elsewhere. Dormitory beds from €16, doubles €45.

International Youth Hostel Europa Baron Ruzettelaan 143 ☎050 35 26 79, ⊛www.vjh.be. Big, modern HI-affiliated hostel in its own grounds, a (dreary) 2km south of the centre in the suburb of Assebroek. There are over two hundred beds in a mixture of rooms from singles through to six-bed dorms. Breakfast is included in the price, and there are also security lockers and internet access, and no curfew. City bus #2 from the train station goes within 150m – ask the driver to let you off. Dorm beds €15, doubles €34.

Passage Dweersstraat 26 ☎050 34 02 32, ⊛www.passagebruges.com. The most agreeable hostel in Bruges, accommodating fifty people in ten comparatively comfortable dormitories (all with shared bathrooms). It's located in an old and interesting part of town, about ten minutes' walk west of the Markt. Closed Jan. Dorm beds from €14 including sheets; €5 extra for breakfast.

Ghent

Ghent has around thirty hotels, ranging from the delightful to the mundanely modern, with several of the most stylish and enjoyable – but not necessarily the most expensive – located in the centre, which is where you want to be. The city also has a good supply of budget accommodation, principally a bright, cheerful and centrally located youth hostel and a modest range of B&Bs, a list of which can be obtained from the tourist office – reckon on €50–70 per double.

Staff at the tourist office (see p.155) in the Lakenhalle will make hotel and B&B reservations on your behalf at no charge, though they do require a small deposit which is deducted from the final bill. They also publish a free brochure detailing local accommodation, including hotels and hostels (but not B&Bs) along with prices, as well as a separate bed and breakfast leaflet – or check out ⓦwww .bedandbreakfast-gent.be.

Hotels

Best Western Hotel Chamade Koningin Elisabethlaan 3 ☎09 220 15 15, ⓦwww .chamade.be. Standard three-star accommodation in bright, modern bedrooms at this chain hotel, though the building itself – a six-storey block – is a bit of an eyesore. A five-minute walk north of the train station. Doubles €110–130.

Boatel Voorhuitkaal 44 ☎09 267 10 30, ⓦwww.theboatel.com. Arguably the most distinctive of the city's hotels, the two-star *Boatel* is, as its name implies, a converted boat – an imaginatively and immaculately refurbished canal barge to be precise. It's moored in one of the city's outer canals, a ten-to-fifteen-minute walk east from the centre. The seven bedrooms are decked out in crisp modern style, and breakfasts, taken on the poop deck, are first rate. Doubles €110–130.

Erasmus Poel 25 ☎09 224 21 95, ⓦwww.erasmushotel.be. Another contender for Ghent's most distinctive hotel, this friendly family-run affair occupies a commodious old town house a few metres from the Korenlei. Each room is thoughtfully decorated and furnished with antiques, and the breakfast is excellent. Reservations strongly advised in summer. Two stars, but this rating does it precious little justice. Doubles €100–150.

Flandre Poel 1 ☎09 266 06 00, ⓦwww .hoteldeflandre.be. The new kid on Ghent's hotel block, this smooth and polished four-star hotel occupies an imaginatively refashioned old coach house a short walk from the Korenmarkt. Spacious public areas kitted out in sharp modern style are followed by neat and trim bedrooms. Doubles €160–240.

Gravensteen Jan Breydelstraat 35 ☎09 225 11 50, ⓦwww.gravensteen.be. In

a great location close to Het Gravensteen, this medium-sized three-star is centred on an attractively restored nineteenth-century mansion adorned with Second Empire trimmings. The rooms in the annexe and in one wing of the original building are smart and relatively spacious, with pleasing modern furnishings. Several of the older rooms, however, are very poky. Doubles €90–190.

Ibis Centrum Kathedraal Limburgstraat 2 ☎09 233 00 00, ⓦwww.ibishotel.com. Handily situated opposite the cathedral, this large two-star – part of the Ibis chain – offers comfortable modern rooms, though the noise from the square in front of the hotel can be irritating late at night – ask for a room at the back. Doubles €75–85.

Ibis Centrum Opera Nederkouter 24–26 ☎09 225 07 07, ⓦwww.ibishotel.com. Spick-and-span modern two-star in a five-storey block a short walk south of the Korenmarkt. The rooms lack character, but they're perfectly adequate and comfortable. Doubles €70–80.

Monasterium Poortackere Oude Houtlei 56 ☎09 269 22 10, ⓦwww .monasterium.be. This unusual two-star hotel-cum-guesthouse occupies a rambling and somewhat spartan former monastery, whose ageing brickwork dates from the nineteenth century. Guests have a choice between the unassuming, en-suite rooms in the hotel section, or opting for a more authentic monastic-cell experience in the guesthouse (some of whose rooms have shared facilities). The complex also includes a pint-sized neo-Gothic chapel, and breakfast is taken in the old chapterhouse. It's about five minutes' walk west of Veldstraat. Doubles €70–115.

Novotel Centrum Goudenleeuwplein 5 ☎09 224 22 30, ⓦwww.novotel.com. First-class modern chain hotel bang in the middle of the town centre. Rooms are neat, trim and fetchingly decorated, and there's also an outdoor swimming pool and good breakfasts. Three star. Doubles €175.

Sofitel Gent Belfort Hoogpoort 63 ☎09 233 33 31, ⓦwww.sofitel.com. One of the plushest hotels in town, this four-star is daintily shoehorned behind an ancient facade across from the Stadhuis. There are spacious, pastel-shaded rooms and suites

ACCOMMODATION

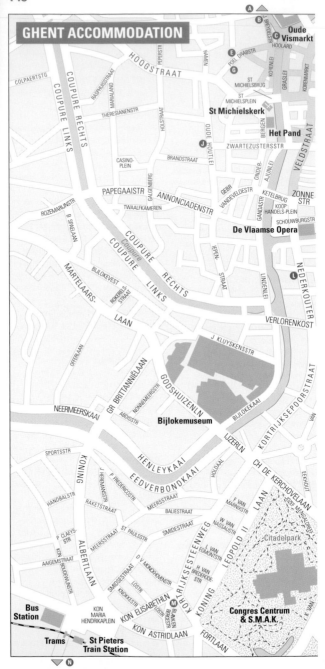

GHENT ACCOMMODATION

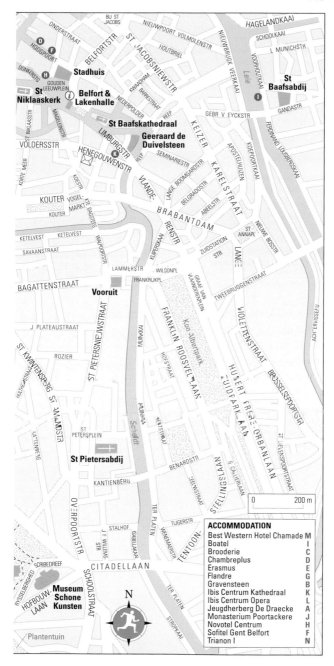

ACCOMMODATION

Best Western Hotel Chamade	M
Boatel	I
Brooderie	C
Chambreplus	D
Erasmus	E
Flandre	G
Gravensteen	B
Ibis Centrum Kathedraal	K
Ibis Centrum Opera	L
Jeugdherberg De Draecke	A
Monasterium Poortackere	J
Novotel Centrum	H
Sofitel Gent Belfort	F
Trianon I	N

as well as all modcons, including good fitness facilities. Enquire direct for discounts. Doubles €200–250.

Trianon I Sint Denijslaan 203 ☎ 09 221 39 44, ⊛ www.hoteltrianon.be. Two-star, motel-style accommodation on a quiet residential street about 2km south of the centre, just beyond Ghent St Pieters train station. The nineteen rooms are comfortable and spotless, and all are en suite. Doubles €60–70.

B&Bs and hostel

Brooderie Jan Breydelstraat 8 ☎ 09 225 06 23, ⊛ www.brooderie.be. Three neat and trim little rooms immediately above the appealing little *Brooderie* café (see p.125). Handily located near the Korenmarkt, and breakfast is excellent. Doubles €60–65.

Chambreplus Hoogpoort 31 ☎ 09 225 37 75, ⊛ www.chambreplus.be. Charming B&B with three extremely cosy, air-conditioned guest rooms – one decorated in the manner of a sultan's room, another in the style of colonial Africa, while the third occupies a self-contained mini-house at the back of the garden. Breakfasts are delicious – as are the home-made chocolates. Smashing central location, too. Doubles €80–95, garden mini-house €155.

Jeugdherberg De Draecke St Widostraat 11 ☎ 09 233 70 50, ⊛ www.vjh.be. Excellent, well-equipped HI-affiliated youth hostel in the city centre, a five-minute walk north of the Korenmarkt with over a hundred beds in two- to six-bed rooms and dorms. Advance reservations are advised, especially in the height of the season. Breakfast is included, and the restaurant offers lunch and dinner too. There are also lockers, a bar, and facilities for bike rental and currency exchange. Dorm beds €17, doubles €44.

Essentials

Arrival

Bruges and Ghent are easy to reach by road and rail. The **E40 motorway**, linking Brussels with Ostend, runs just to the south of both cities, and there are fast and frequent **trains** to Ghent and Bruges from Brussels and a batch of other Belgian cities. Long-distance **international buses** also run direct to Bruges and Ghent from a number of capital cities, including London, and there are **car ferries** from Rosyth and Hull to Zeebrugge, a few kilometres from Bruges. The nearest airport to both cities is Brussels. There are three trains an hour between Bruges and Ghent; the journey time is twenty minutes.

In **Bruges**, the train and bus station are next to one another about 2km south-west of the city centre. If the flat and easy twenty minute walk into the centre doesn't appeal, most of the local buses leaving from outside the train station head off to the main square, the Markt, with some services stopping on the square itself and others stopping on adjacent Wollestraat, both bang in the centre. All local buses have destination signs at the front, but if in doubt check with the driver. A taxi from the train station to the centre should cost about €8.

Ghent has three train stations, but the biggest by far – and the one you're almost bound to arrive at – is Ghent St Pieters, which adjoins the bus station some 2km south of the city centre. From the west side of St Pieters train station, tram #1 runs up to the Korenmarkt, right in the city centre, every few minutes, passing along Kortrijksepoortstraat and Nederkouter. All trams have destination signs and numbers at the front, but if in doubt check with the driver. The taxi fare from the train station to the Korenmarkt is about €8.

By air

The nearest airport to Bruges and Ghent is **Brussels international airport**. From the airport, there are three or four trains every hour to Brussels' three main stations: Bruxelles-Nord, Bruxelles-Centrale and Bruxelles-Midi. The journey time to Bruxelles-Nord is about twenty minutes; a few minutes more to the others. You can change at any of these stations for the twice-hourly train from Brussels to Bruges and Ghent, though changing at Bruxelles-Nord is a tad more convenient since it isn't as crowded as the other two. The journey from Brussels takes an hour to Bruges, forty minutes to Ghent. There are also direct trains from the airport to Ghent (1–2 hourly), from where there are onward connections to Bruges (3 hourly; 20min), but this isn't much quicker. The one-way **fare** from Brussels' airport to Bruges is currently €13.20, exactly twice that for a return; the fare to Ghent is slightly less.

Note that some flights to Brussels (including Ryanair services) land at **Brussels (Charleroi) airport**, well to the south of the capital and an hour or so away from Brussels by bus.

By train

Bruges and Ghent are very well served by train (Ⓦ www.b-rail.be), with fast and frequent services from a number of Belgian towns and cities including Brussels and Ostend. Trains from Brussels to Bruges and Ghent depart from all three of the capital's mainline stations including Bruxelles-Midi, the terminus of Eurostar trains from London. **Eurostar** trains (Ⓦ www.eurostar.com) take two hours to get from London St Pancras to Bruxelles-Midi station, from where it's another hour or so by domestic train to get to Bruges, forty minutes to Ghent. Bruxelles-Midi station is also served by **Thalys** (Ⓦ www.thalys.com) international express trains from Amsterdam, Cologne, Aachen and Paris. Some of the Thalys trains from Paris continue on to Ostend via Ghent and Bruges.

By car

To reach Belgium by car or motorbike, you can either take one of the car ferries mentioned above or use **Eurotunnel's shuttle train** through the Channel Tunnel from near Folkestone (exit the M20 at junction 11a). Note that Eurotunnel only carries cars (including occupants) and motorbikes, not cyclists and foot passengers. From the Eurotunnel exit in Calais, it's just 120km to Bruges and 200km to Brussels.

Bruges is clearly signed from the E40 motorway, and its oval-shaped centre is encircled by the R30 ring road, which follows the course of the old city walls. **Parking** in the centre can be a real tribulation, with on-street parking almost impossible to find and the city centre's handful of car parks often filled to the gunnels. Easily the best option is to use the massive 24/7 car park by the train station, particularly as the price – €2.50 per day – includes the cost of the bus ride to and from the centre.

Ghent is also well signed from the E40 motorway and encircled by a ring road. **Car parks** within the city centre are often jam-packed; the city has signed two parking routes (*parkeerroute*), one signed with yellow arrows (anti-clockwise), the other with green (clockwise). Both lead to – or past – the nine car parks that lie in or close to the centre. The green route is better for the central car parks and is a little less convoluted than the other; the 24-hour car park beneath the Vrijdagmarkt is one of the best placed.

By ferry

Three operators currently run **car ferries** from the UK direct to Belgium. These are Transeuropa Ferries (Ramsgate to Ostend; 4hr; ⓦ www.transeuropaferries .com); P&O Ferries (Hull to Zeebrugge; 13hr; ⓦ www.poferries.com); and Superfast Ferries (Rosyth to Zeebrugge; 18hr; ⓦ www.superfast.com). Both Zeebrugge and Ostend are within easy striking distance of Bruges and Ghent. Tariffs vary enormously, depending on when you leave, how long you stay, what size your vehicle is and how many passengers are in it; on the two longer routes, there's also the cost of a cabin to consider and booking ahead is strongly recommended – indeed essential in summer.

Entry requirements

Citizens of all EU and EEA countries only need a valid **passport** or **national identity card** to enter Belgium, where – with some limitations – they also have the right to work, live and study. US, Australian, Canadian, South African and New Zealand citizens need only a valid passport for visits of up to ninety days, but are not allowed to work. Passports must be valid for at least three months beyond the period of intended stay. Non-EU citizens who wish to visit Belgium for longer than ninety days must get a special **visa** from a Belgian consulate or embassy before departure. Visa requirements do change and it is always advisable to check the current situation before leaving home.

Information

Bruges has two tourist offices. There's a **tourist information desk** (Tues–Sat 9.30am–12.30pm & 1–5pm) inside the train station, next to the ticket office, while the main **tourist office** (daily 10am–6pm, Thurs till 8pm; ☎ 050 44 46 46, ⓦ www.brugge.be) is in the Concertgebouw complex on the west side of the city centre on 't Zand. Among a variety of free leaflets, there's a comprehensive accommodation listings brochure and a bi-monthly, multilingual events booklet, though the latter isn't nearly as detailed as *Exit* (ⓦ www.exit .be), a free monthly, Dutch-language newssheet available here and at many town-centre bars, cafés and bookshops.

In **Ghent**, the **tourist office** is bang in the centre of the city in the crypt of the Lakenhalle (daily: April–Oct 9.30am–6.30pm; Nov–March 9.30am–4.30pm; ☎ 09 266 56 60, ⓦ www.visitgent .be). They supply a wide range of free city information as does Ghent's **youth tourist information office**, Use-it, at St Pietersnieuwstraat 21 (Mon–Fri 1–6pm; ⓦ www.use-it.be).

City transport

The most enjoyable way to explore Bruges is on foot, and the centre is certainly compact and flat enough to make this an easy proposition. The same applies in Ghent, except that here some of the more outlying attractions are best reached by tram. Both cities have excellent **public transport** systems, with buses and trams in Ghent and buses in Bruges running to every suburban nook and cranny. All services are operated by De Lijn (☎ 070 22 02 00, ⓦ www .delijn.be), who have information kiosks outside Bruges and Ghent St Pieters train stations. Tickets are widely available at shops and newsagents and at the automatic ticket machines at major stops, including the two train stations mentioned above. Note that at peak times some tram and bus drivers won't issue tickets. The standard single **fare** is €1.20 in advance, or €1.50 from the driver; a ten-journey Lijnkaart costs €8 in advance, or €10 from the driver; and a 24-hour city bus pass, called a *dagpas*, costs €5, or €6 from the driver. Free maps of the local network are available at the information kiosks.

Cycling

Bruges is ideal for cycling, with cycle lanes on many of the roads, and cycle racks dotted across the centre. There are half a dozen bike rental places in Bruges, but Belgian Railways sets the benchmark, hiring out bikes at the railway station

Boat trips

Half-hour boat trips around Bruges's central canals leave from a number of jetties south of the Burg (March–Nov daily 10am–6pm; €5.70). Boats depart every few minutes, but long queues still build up during high season, with few visitors seemingly concerned by the canned commentary. In wintertime (Dec–Feb), there's a spasmodic service at weekends only. There are also boat excursions out from Bruges to the attractive town of Damme (see p.104), as well as boat trips around Ghent's central canals (see p.110).

Guided tours

Guided tours are big business in **Bruges**; the main tourist office (see p.155) has comprehensive details. All sorts of tours are offered, from horse-and-carriage rides to boat trips, as well as excursions out into the Flemish countryside, most notably to the battlefields of World War I.

Among the many options, Sightseeing Line (☎050 35 50 24, ⊛www.citytour .be) operates fifty-minute **mini-coach tours** (€11.50 per adult; pay the driver) of the city centre, departing from the Markt; passengers are issued with individual headphones in the language of their choice. More expensive are the **horse-drawn carriages**, which line up on the Markt offering a thirty-minute canter round town for €30. These are extremely popular, so expect to queue at the weekend. Bruges has a small army of tour operators, but one of the best is **Quasimodo Tours** (☎050 37 04 70, ⊛www.quasimodo.be), who run a first-rate programme of excursions both in and around Bruges and out into Flanders. Their laid-back **Flanders Fields** minibus tour (7hr 30min) of the World War I battlefields near Ieper is highly recommended; tours cost €50 (under-26s €40) including picnic lunch. Reservations are required and hotel or train station pick-up can be arranged. Their sister organization, **Quasimundo** (☎050 33 07 75, ⊛www.quasimundo.be) runs several **bike tours**, starting from the Burg. Their "Bruges by Bike" excursion (daily March–Oct; 2.5hr; €22) zips round the main sights and then explores less visited parts of the city, while their "Border by Bike" tour (daily March–Oct; 4hr; €22) comprises a 25-kilometre ride out along the poplar-lined canals to the north of Bruges, visiting Damme and Oostkerke with stops and stories along the way. Both are good fun and the price includes mountain bike and rain-jacket hire; reservations are required.

In **Ghent**, guided **walking tours** are particularly popular. The standard walking tour, organized by the tourist office, consists of a two-hour jaunt round the city centre (May–Oct daily at 2.30pm; Nov–April Sat at 2.30pm; €7); bookings – at least a few hours in advance – are strongly recommended. Alternatively, **horse-drawn carriages** leave from outside the Lakenhalle, on St Baafsplein, offering a thirty-minute gambol round town for €25 (April–Oct daily 10am–6pm & most winter weekends).

(☎050 30 23 29; €9.50 per day). The main tourist office (see p.155) issues a useful free leaflet detailing five cycle routes in the countryside around Bruges, while Quasimundo Tours offer guided cycling tours (see above).

Ghent is good for cycling too: the terrain is flat and there are cycle lanes on many of the roads and cycle racks dotted across the centre. There are a couple of bike rental outlets in Ghent; again, Belgian Railways should be your first port of call, with bikes for hire at St Pieters railway station (☎09 241 22 24; daily 7am–8pm; €9.50 per day).

Car rental

Car rental companies are surprisingly thin on the ground in Bruges. Operators include Europcar, at St Pieterskaai 48 (☎050 31 45 44), and Hertz, at Pathoekeweg 25 (☎050 37 72 34). In both cases, advance reservations are advised, especially in summer. Ghent is better equipped – try Avis, Kortrijksesteenweg 676 (☎09 222 00 53); Europcar, Einde Were 1 (☎09 226 81 26); or Hertz, Nieuwewandeling 76 (☎09 224 04 06).

Performing arts and cinema

Keen to entertain its many visitors, **Bruges** puts on a varied programme of performing arts, mostly as part of its annual schedule of festivals and special events (see p.158). The two principal venues are the municipal theatre, the Stadsschouwburg, and the city's prestigious concert hall, the Concertgebouw.

Listings of forthcoming events are posted on the tourist office website at Ⓦ www.brugge.bc. The main tourist office, on 't Zand (see p.155), also publishes a free – if somewhat skimpy – multilingual events calendar called *evenementen*, supplemented by their rather more detailed monthly *events@brugge*. The much more detailed local listings magazine *Exit* (Ⓦ www.exit.be) is also published monthly and has in-depth reviews and a calendar. It's widely available in bookshops and assorted outlets, including the tourist office, but is (almost entirely) in Dutch.

In **Ghent**, the performing arts are geared up for the local citizenry rather than the city's visitors. For the low-down on upcoming events in Ghent, either ask at the tourist office (see p.155) or check out their website Ⓦ www.visitgent .be). The city's best **listings** magazine is the fortnightly freebie *Zone 09* (Ⓦ www .zone09.be); it's available at newspaper stands all over the city centre. The FNAC bookshop (see p.137) sells tickets for most mainstream cultural events.

Cinema

Films are normally shown in the original language, with Dutch subtitles as required.

In Bruges

Ciné Liberty Kuipersstraat 23 ☎ 050 33 20 11, Ⓦ www.cinebel.be. Located right in the centre of town in an attractive old building and screening a choice selection of arthouse and mainstream English and American films.

Cinema Lumière St-Jacobstraat 36 ☎ 050 34 34 65, Ⓦ www.lumiere.be. Bruges's premier venue for alternative, cult, foreign and art-house movies, with three screens.

In Ghent

Sphinx St-Michielshelling 3 ☎ 09 225 60 86, Ⓦ www.sphinx-cinema.be. Popular cinema which focuses on foreign-language and art-house films.
Studio Skoop St-Annaplein 63 ☎ 09 225 08 45, Ⓦ www.studioskoop.be. The cosiest of the city's cinemas, with five screens.

Classical music, opera, theatre and dance

In Bruges

Collegium Instrumentale Brugense ☎ 050 81 66 18, Ⓦ www .collegiuminstrumentale.be. Based in Bruges, this internationally acclaimed chamber orchestra gives fairly frequent performances in a variety of local venues. Performances dip into many historical periods, but focus principally on the Baroque.
Concertgebouw 't Zand ☎ 070 22 33 02, Ⓦ www.concertgebouw.be. Built to celebrate Bruges's year as a cultural capital of Europe in 2002, the Concertgebouw (Concert Hall) hosts a range of performing arts, from opera and classical music through to big-name bands.
Stadsschouwburg Vlamingstraat 29 ☎ 050 44 30 60, Ⓦ www.cultuurcentrumbrugge .be. Occupying a big and breezy, neo-Renaissance building dating from 1869, the Stadsschouwburg (Municipal Theatre) hosts a wide-ranging programme of theatre, dance, musicals, concerts and opera.

In Ghent

Concertzaal Handelsbeurs Kouter 29 ☎ 09 265 91 60, Ⓦ www.handelsbeurs .be. The city's newest concert hall with two first-rate auditoria, hosting a diverse programme spanning all the performing arts.

Publiekstheater Groot Huis St-Baafsplein 17 ☎09 225 01 01, ⒲www.publiekstheater.be. Handsomely restored nineteenth-century theatre hosting a wide range of performing arts events. It's home to Nederlands Toneel Gent (☎09 225 01 01, ⒲www.ntgent.be), the regional repertory company, whose performances are almost always in Dutch, though the theatre also plays occasional host to touring English-language theatre companies.

De Vlaamse Opera Schouwburgstraat 3 ☎09 268 10 11, ⒲www.vlaamseopera.be. The lavishly restored opera house is home to the city's opera company.

Vooruit St-Pietersnieuwstraat 23 ☎09 267 28 28, ⒲www.vooruit.be. Ghent's leading venue for rock, pop and jazz concerts; also stages modern dance and theatre.

Festivals and events

Bruges and Ghent are big on festivals and special events – everything from religious processions through to cinema, fairs and contemporary musical binges. These are spread throughout the year, though (as you might expect) most tourist-oriented events take place in the summer. Information on upcoming festivals and events is easy to come by either from the main tourist offices and their websites (see p.155) or from the various listings publications covered on p.157.

March

Cinema Novo (Bruges) Held over eleven days in March, the prestigious Cinema Novo film festival (⒲www.cinemanovo.be) aims to establish a European foothold for films from Africa, Asia and Latin America. Most are shown at the city's art-house cinemas (see p.157).

April

Meifoor (Bruges) Late April to late May; ☎050/44 80 41, ⒲www.brugge.be. Bruges's main annual funfair, held on 't Zand and in the adjoining Koning Albertpark.

May

Festival van Vlaanderen (Flanders Festival) (Bruges and Ghent) May–Oct across Flanders; ⒲www.festival-van-vlaanderen.be. For well over forty years, the Flanders Festival has provided classical music in churches, castles and other impressive venues in over sixty Flemish towns and cities. The festival now comprises more than 120 concerts and features international orchestras. Each of the big Dutch-speaking cities – including Ghent and Bruges – gets a fair crack of the cultural whip, with the festival celebrated for about two weeks in each city before it moves on to the next.

Heilig Bloedprocessie (Procession of the Holy Blood) (Bruges) Ascension Day (forty days after Easter); ☎05 044 86 86, ⒲www.holyblood.org. One of medieval Christendom's holiest relics, the phial of the Holy Blood, said to contain a few drops of the blood of Christ, is carried through the centre of Bruges once every year. Nowadays, the procession is as much a tourist attraction as a religious ceremony, but it remains an important event for many citizens of Bruges.

July

Cactusfestival (Bruges) Three days over the second weekend of July; ⒲www.cactusmusic.be. Going strong for over twenty years, the Cactusfestival is something of a classic. Known for its amiable atmosphere, it proudly pushes against the musical mainstream with rock, reggae, rap, roots and R&B all rolling along together. The festival features both domestic and foreign artists – recent show-stoppers have included Elvis Costello, Patti Smith and Richard Thompson. It's held in Bruges's city centre, in the park beside the Minnewater.

Gentse Feesten (Ghent Festival) Mid-to late July, but always including July 21; ⒲www.gentsefeesten.be. For ten days every July, Ghent gets stuck into partying pretty much round the clock. Local bands perform free open-air gigs throughout the city and street performers turn up all over the place – fire-eaters, buskers, comedians, actors, puppeteers and so forth. There's also an outdoor market

Public holidays

New Year's Day
Easter Monday
Labour Day (May 1)
Ascension Day (forty days after Easter)
Whit Monday
Flemish Day (Dutch-speaking
   Belgium only; July 11)
Belgium National Day (July 21)
Assumption (mid-August)
All Saints' Day (November 1)
Armistice Day (November 11)
Christmas Day

(Note that if any one of the above
falls on a Sunday, the next day
becomes a holiday.)

selling everything from *jenever* (gin) to
handmade crafts.
Klinkers (Bruges) Two and a half weeks,
usually from the last weekend of July,
@www.cactusmusic.be. Bruges's biggest
annual knees-up, and the chance for city
folk to really let their hair down. There are
big-time concerts on the Markt and the
Burg, the city's two main squares, more
intimate performances in various bars and
cafés, and film screenings in Astrid Park,
plus all sorts of other entertainments. It's
Bruges at its best — and most of the
events are free.
**Knokke-Heist: Internationaal Cartoon-
festival (near Bruges)** Late July to early
Sept; @cartoonfestival.otr.be. Established in
the 1960s, this summer-season festival in
the seaside resort of Knokke-Heist, a short
train ride from Bruges, showcases several
hundred world-class cartoons drawn in and
from every corner of the globe.
Musica Antiqua (Bruges) Last week of
July and first week of Aug; @www.musica
-antiqua.com. Part of the Festival van
Vlaanderen (see opposite), this well-
established and well-regarded festival of
medieval music offers an extensive
programme of live performances at a
variety of historic venues in Bruges. The
evening concerts are built around themes,
whilst the lunchtime concerts are more
episodic. Tickets go on sale in Feb and are
snapped up fast.

August

Sand sculpture (near Bruges) Aug to late
Sept Sand-sculpture competitions are popular along the Belgian coast throughout the
summer – and Zeebrugge, a few minutes by
train from Bruges, features some of the most
amazing creations.
**Praalstoet van de Gouden Boom
(Pageant of the Golden Tree) (Bruges)**
Held every five years over two days on
the last weekend of August, this pageant
features all sorts of mock-medieval hearti-
ness, and thousands congregate in central
Bruges to join in the fun. First staged in
1958, the next one is due in 2012.

October

Ghent Film Festival Held over twelve days
in October, the Ghent Film Festival (@www
.filmfestival.be) is one of Europe's foremost
cinematic events. Every year, the city's
art-house cinemas (see p.157) combine
to present a total of around two hundred
feature films and a hundred shorts from all
over the world, screening Belgian films and
the best of world cinema well before they
hit the international circuit. There's also a
special focus on music in film.

November

**Zesdaagse an Vlaanderen (The Six
Days of Flanders Cycling Event) (Ghent)**
@www.kuipke.be. Held over six days in
mid-Nov, this annual cycling extravaganza
takes place in the vélodrome at the Citadelpark in Ghent and attracts cyclists from all
over Europe, who thrash around for dear life
in six days of high-speed racing.

December

**The Arrival of St Nicholas (aka Santa
Klaus) (Bruges and Ghent)** Dec 6. The
arrival of St Nicholas from his long sojourn
abroad is celebrated by processions and
the giving of sweets to children right
across Belgium.
**Kerstmarkt (Christmas Market)
(Bruges).** Dec daily 11am–10pm. All Dec
Bruges's Christmas Market occupies the
Markt with scores of brightly lit stalls selling food, drink, souvenirs and everything
Christmassy. The centre of the Markt is
turned into an ice rink and you can rent
skates. There's more Christmas jollity at the
comparable Christmas Market on the Simon
Stevinplein (daily 11am–7pm).

Directory

ATMs ATMs are liberally distributed across the centre of both Bruges and Ghent. In Bruges there are handy ATMs at the post office, Markt 5; KBC, Steenstraat 38; Fortis Bank, Simon Stevinplein 3; AXA, 't Zand 1; and the Europabank, Vlamingstraat 13. In Ghent, there are useful ATMs on the Groentenmarkt; the Vrijdagmarkt; and the Kouter.

Currency and exchange The Belgian currency is the euro (€). Each euro is made up of 100 cents. At time of writing the rate of exchange for €1 was £0.67, US$1.35, CDN$1.45, AUS$1.60, NZ$1.75, SAR9.56. For the most up-to-date rates, ⓦwww .oanda.com

Beaches About 70km from tip to toe, the Belgian coast boasts mile upon mile of sandy beach. The seaside resorts of Ostend, Blankenberge and Knokke-Heist are all a short train ride from Bruges – and not much further by train from Ghent.

Disabilities, Travellers with Bruges and Ghent are not particularly well equipped to accommodate travellers with disabilities. Lifts and ramps are comparatively rare, buses, trams and trains are not routinely accessible for wheelchair users, and rough pavements are commonplace and obstacles frequent. That said, attitudes have changed: most new buildings are required to be fully accessible and the number of premises geared up for the disabled traveller has increased dramatically in the last few years. Consequently, finding a hotel with wheelchair access and other appropriate facilities is not too difficult. For specific advice, contact the local tourist offices (see p.155).

Electricity In Belgium, the current is 220V AC, with standard European-style two-pin plugs. British equipment needs only a plug adaptor; American apparatus requires a transformer and an adaptor.

Emergencies Fire and ambulance ☎100, police ☎101.

Football Founded in 1891, Club Brugge (ⓦwww.clubbrugge.be) is the premier soccer club in the province of Flanders and a recent winner of the Belgian league and cup. They play in the Jan Breydelstadion, a 10min drive southwest from the centre of Bruges along Gistelse Steenweg; on match days there are special buses to the ground from the train station. Match tickets cost between €15 and €50.

Internet and email access In both Bruges and Ghent, most hotels and hostels provide internet access for their guests either free or at minimal charge. There are also several internet cafés in both cities. In Bruges, the most central is The Coffee Link, in the Oud St-Jan shopping centre off Mariastraat (daily except Thurs & Fri 11am–6pm; ☎050 34 99 73, ⓦwww .thecoffeelink.com). Rates are currently €0.20 per minute, after an initial charge of €2 for the first ten minutes. In Ghent, the handiest internet café is the Coffee Lounge, across from the tourist office at Botermarkt 6 (daily 10am–7pm).

Left luggage There are luggage lockers and a luggage office at Bruges train station and at Ghent St Pieters train station.

Pharmacies There are plenty of pharmacies in both Bruges and Ghent and late-night duty rotas are usually displayed in pharmacists' windows. In Bruges, you can also check which pharmacies are open late-night and at weekends by calling ☎050 40 61 62.

Phones There are no area codes in Belgium and there's no distinction between local and long-distance calls – in other words calling Brussels from Bruges costs the same as calling a number within Bruges. To call Belgium from abroad, dial your international access code, then ☎32 (the country code for Belgium), followed by the subscriber number minus its initial zero. To make an international phone call

Fly Less – Stay Longer!

Rough Guides believes in the good that travel does, but we are deeply aware of the impact of fuel emissions on climate change. We recommend taking fewer trips and staying for longer. If you can avoid travelling by air, please use an alternative, especially for journeys of under 1000km/600miles. And always offset your travel at ⓦwww.roughguides.com/climatechange.

from within Belgium, dial ☎00 followed by the appropriate international access code (see below), then the number you require, omitting the initial zero where there is one. International codes include Australia ☎61; Canada ☎1; Republic of Ireland ☎353; New Zealand ☎64; South Africa ☎27; UK ☎44; and USA ☎1. For domestic directory enquiries within Flanders, call ☎1207; international directory enquiries and operator assistance are on ☎1204. Telephone numbers beginning ☎0900 or ☎070 are premium-rated, ☎0800 are toll-free.

All but the remotest parts of Belgium have mobile (cellphone) coverage; GSM phones from the rest of Europe, Australia and New Zealand should work fine; those bought in North America (apart from triband cellphones) won't.

Post office Bruges: Markt 5 (Mon–Fri 9am–5.30pm); Ghent: Lange Kruisstraat 55 (Mon–Fri 9am–6pm, Sat 9am–12.30pm).

Stilettos Very few local women wear high heels in either Ghent or Bruges because they get stuck in between the cobble stones.

Taxis In Bruges, there's a taxi rank on the Markt (☎050 33 44 44) and another outside the train station on Stationsplein (☎050 38 46 60). In Ghent, taxis queue up outside Ghent St Pieters train station, or call V-Tax (☎09 222 22 22).

Time Belgium is on Central European Time (CET), one hour ahead of Greenwich Mean Time, six hours ahead of US Eastern Standard Time, nine hours ahead of US Pacific Standard Time, nine hours behind Australian Eastern Standard Time, and eleven hours behind New Zealand – except for periods during the changeovers made in the respective countries to and from daylight saving. Belgium operates daylight saving, moving clocks forward one hour in the spring and one hour back in the autumn.

Tipping Tipping is, of course, never obligatory, but a ten- to fifteen-percent tip is expected by taxi drivers and anticipated by most restaurant waiters.

Toilets Public toilets remain comparatively rare, but some cafés and bars run what amounts to an ablutionary sideline with (mostly middle-aged) women keeping the toilets scrupulously clean and making a minimal charge, though this custom is fizzling out. Where it still applies, you'll spot the plate for the money as you enter.

Train enquiries For domestic and international services, either drop by the nearest train station or call ☎050 30 24 24 (daily 7am–9pm; ⓦ www.b-rail.be).

Chronology

Chronology

630 ▶ The French missionary St Amand establishes an abbey on the site of present-day Ghent, at the confluence of the rivers Leie and Scheldt.

865 ▶ Bruges founded as a coastal stronghold against the Vikings by Baldwin Iron Arm, first count of Flanders.

Tenth century ▶ The beginnings of the wool industry in Flanders. The leading Flemish cloth towns are Bruges and Ghent.

Twelfth to late fourteenth century ▶ The Flemish cloth industry becomes dependent on English wool. Flanders enjoys an unprecedented economic boom and its merchants become immensely rich. Increasing tension – and bouts of warfare – between the merchants and weavers of Flanders and their feudal overlords, the counts of Flanders and the kings of France. Ghent becomes the seat of the counts of Flanders and the largest town in western Europe.

1302 ▶ Bruges Matins, when the citizens of Bruges massacre a French garrison: anyone who couldn't correctly pronounce the Flemish shibboleth *schild en vriend* ("shield and friend") was put to the sword.

1384 ▶ The dukes of Burgundy inherit Flanders.

1419 ▶ Philip the Good, Duke of Burgundy, makes Bruges his capital. The Burgundian court becomes known across Europe for its cultured opulence. Philip dies in 1467.

1482 ▶ Mary, the last of the Burgundians, dies and her territories – including Flanders – revert to her husband, Maximilian, a Habsburg prince. Thus, Flanders is absorbed into the Habsburg empire.

1480s onwards ▶ Decline of the Flemish cloth industry.

1530s ▶ Bruges's international trade collapses and the town slips into a long decline. Ghent also experiences a decline, though its merchants switch from industry to trade, keeping the city going – if not exactly flourishing.

Mid-sixteenth to seventeenth century ▶ The Protestants of the Low Countries (modern-day Belgium and the Netherlands) rebel against their Catholic Habsburg kings. A long and cruel series of wars ensues. Eventually, the Netherlands wins its independence – as the United Provinces – and the south, including Flanders, is reconstituted as the Spanish Netherlands.

1700 ▶ The last of the Spanish Habsburgs, Charles II, dies; the War of the Spanish Succession follows.

1713 ▶ The Treaty of Utrecht passes what is now Belgium, including Flanders, to the Austrians – as the Austrian Netherlands.

1794 ▶ Napoleon occupies the Austrian Netherlands and annexes it to France the following year.

1815 ▶ Napoleon is defeated at Waterloo, just south of Brussels, and the Austrian Netherlands becomes half of the newly constituted Kingdom of The Netherlands.

1830 ▶ A rebellion leads to the collapse of the new kingdom and the creation of an independent Belgium, including Flanders.

Mid- to late nineteenth century ▶ Much of Belgium industrializes, including Ghent but not Bruges, whose antique charms attract a first wave of tourists.

1913 ▶ The Great Exhibition, showing the best in contemporary design and goods, is staged in Ghent.

1914–1945 ▶ Bruges and Ghent are occupied by the Germans in both world wars, but survive largely unscathed.

1950s ▶ Increasing tension between the French- and Dutch-speaking regions of Belgium.

1980 ▶ Belgium is divided into three federal regions: Wallonia for French-speakers; Brussels, which is designated as bilingual; and Dutch-speaking Flanders, including the two provinces of East and West Flanders (Ghent is in East Flanders, Bruges in West).

Language

Language

Throughout the northern part of Belgium, including West Flanders – which covers Bruges and Ghent – the principal language is Dutch, which is spoken in a variety of distinctive dialects commonly described as "Flemish". Dutch-speaking Belgians commonly refer to themselves as Flemish-speakers and most of them, particularly in the tourist industry, also speak English to varying degrees of excellence. Indeed, Flemish-speakers have a seemingly natural talent for languages, and your attempts at speaking theirs may be met with bewilderment – though this can have as much to do with your pronunciation (Dutch is very difficult to get right) as surprise you're making the effort.

Consequently, the following words and phrases should be the most you'll need to get by. We've also included a basic **food and drink** glossary, though menus are nearly always multilingual; where they aren't, ask and one will almost invariably appear.

As for **phrasebooks**, the pocket-sized *Rough Guide to Dutch* has a good dictionary section (English–Dutch and Dutch–English) as well as a menu reader; it also provides a useful introduction to grammar and pronunciation.

Pronunciation

Dutch is **pronounced** much the same as English, though there are a few Dutch sounds that don't exist in English and which can be difficult to get right without practice.

Consonants

j is an English **y**, as in yellow

ch and **g** indicate a throaty sound, as at the end of the Scottish word loch. The Dutch word for canal – *gracht* – is especially tricky, since it has two of these sounds – it comes out sounding something like *khrakht*. A common word for hello is *Dag!* – pronounced like *daakh*

ng as in bring

nj as in onion

y is not a consonant, but another way of writing ij

Double-consonant combinations generally keep their separate sounds in Flemish: **kn**, for example, is never like the English "knight".

Vowels and diphthongs

A good rule of thumb is that doubling the letter lengthens the vowel sound.

a is like the English apple

aa like cart

e like let

ee like late

o as in pop

oo in pope

u is like the French tu if preceded by a consonant; it's like wood if followed by a consonant

uu is like the French tu

au and **ou** like how

ei and **ij** as in fine, though this varies strongly from region to region; sometimes it can sound more like lane

oe as in soon

eu is like the diphthong in the French leur
ui is the hardest Dutch diphthong of all,
   pronounced like how but much further

forward in the mouth, with lips pursed
(as if to say "oo").

Words and phrases

Basic expressions

ja	yes
nee	no
alstublieft	please
dank u or bedankt	thank you
hallo or dag	hello
goedemorgen	good morning
goedemiddag	good afternoon
goedenavond	good evening
tot ziens	goodbye
tot straks	see you later
Spreekt u Engels?	Do you speak English?
Ik begrijp het niet	I don't understand
vrouwen/mannen	women/men
kinderen	children
heren/dames	men's/women's toilets
Ik wil…	I want…
Ik wil niet… (+verb)	I don't want to…
Ik wil geen… (+noun)	I don't want any…
Wat kost…?	How much is…?
sorry	sorry
hier/daar	here/there
goed/slecht	good/bad
groot/klein	big/small
open/gesloten	open/closed
duwen/trekken	push/pull
nieuw/oud	new/old
goedkoop/duur	cheap/expensive
heet or warm/koud	hot/cold
met/zonder	with/without
Hoe kom ik in…?	How do I get to…?
Waar is…?	Where is…?
Hoe ver is het naar…?	How far is it to…?
Wanneer?	When?
ver/dichtbij	far/near
links/rechts	left/right
rechtdoor	straight ahead
alle richtingen	all directions (road sign)
postkantoor	post office
postzegel(s)	stamp(s)
geldwisselkantoor	money exchange
kassa	cash desk
spoor or perron	railway platform
loket	ticket office

Useful cycling terms

fiets	Bicycle
fietspad	bicycle path
band	tyre
lek	puncture
rem	brake
ketting	chain
wiel	wheel
trapper	pedal
pomp	pump
stuur	handlebars
kapot	broken

Numbers

nul	0
een	1
twee	2
drie	3
vier	4
vijf	5
zes	6
zeven	7
acht	8
negen	9
tien	10
elf	11
twaalf	12
dertien	13
veertien	14
vijftien	15
zestien	16
zeventien	17
achttien	18
negentien	19
twintig	20
een en twintig	21
twee en twintig	22
dertig	30
veertig	40
vijftig	50
zestig	60
zeventig	70
tachtig	80
negentig	90
honderd	100

honderd een	101
twee honderd	200
twee honderd een	201
vijf honderd	500
vijf honderd vijf en twintig	525
duizend	1000

mei	May
juni	June
juli	July
augustus	August
september	September
oktober	October
november	November
december	December

Days

maandag	Monday
dinsdag	Tuesday
woensdag	Wednesday
donderdag	Thursday
vrijdag	Friday
zaterdag	Saturday
zondag	Sunday
gisteren	yesterday
vandaag	today
morgen	tomorrow
morgenochtend	tomorrow morning
jaar	year
maand	month
week	week
dag	day

Months

januari	January
februari	February
maart	March
april	April

Time

uur	hour
minuut	minute
Hoe laat is het?	What time is it?
Het is…	It's…
drie uur	3.00
vijf over drie	3.05
tien over drie	3.10
kwart over drie	3.15
tien voor half vier	3.20
vijf voor half vier	3.25
half vier	3.30
vijf over half vier	3.35
tien over half vier	3.40
kwart voor vier	3.45
tien voor vier	3.50
vijf voor vier	3.55
acht uur 's ochtends	8am
een uur 's middags	1pm
acht uur 's avonds	8pm
een uur 's nachts	1am

Food and drink terms

Basic terms and ingredients

belegd	filled or topped, as in belegde broodjes (bread rolls topped with cheese, etc)
boter	butter
boterham/broodje	sandwich/roll
brood	bread
dranken	drinks
eieren	eggs
gerst	barley
groenten	vegetables
Hollandse saus	hollandaise sauce
honing	honey
hoofdgerechten	main courses
kaas	cheese
koud	cold
nagerechten	desserts
peper	pepper

pindakaas	peanut butter
sla/salade	salad
smeerkaas	cheese spread
stokbrood	french bread
suiker	sugar
vis	fish
vlees	meat
voorgerechten	starters/hors d'oeuvres
vruchten	fruit
warm	hot
zout	salt

Cooking methods

doorbakken	well-done
half doorbakken	medium well-done
gebakken	fried or baked
gebraden	roast
gegrild	grilled
gekookt	boiled
geraspt	grated

gerookt	smoked
gestoofd	stewed
rood	rare

Starters and snacks

erwtensoep/snert	thick pea soup with bacon or sausage
huzarensalade	potato salad with pickles
koffietafel	light midday meal of cold meats, cheese, bread, and perhaps soup
patat/friet	chips/french fries
soep	soup
uitsmijter	ham or cheese with eggs on bread

Meat and poultry

biefstuk (hollandse)	steak
biefstuk (duitse)	hamburger
eend	duck
fricandeau	roast pork
fricandel	frankfurter-like sausage
gehakt	minced meat
ham	ham
kalfsvlees	veal
kalkoen	turkey
karbonade	a chop
kip	chicken
kroket	spiced veal or beef in hash, coated in breadcrumbs
lamsvlees	lamb
lever	liver
ossenhaas	tenderloin beef
rookvlees	smoked beef
spek	bacon
worst	sausages

Fish and seafood

forel	trout
garnalen	prawns
haring	herring
haringsalade	herring salad
kabeljauw	cod
makreel	mackerel
mosselen	mussels
oesters	oysters
paling	eel
schelvis	haddock
schol	plaice

tong	sole
zalm	salmon
zeeduivel	monkfish

Vegetables

aardappelen	potatoes
bloemkool	cauliflower
bonen	beans
champignons	mushrooms
erwten	peas
hutspot	mashed potatoes and carrots
knoflook	garlic
komkommer	cucumber
prei	leek
rijst	rice
sla	salad, lettuce
stampot andijvie	mashed potato and endive
stampot boerenkool	mashed potato and cabbage
uien	onions
wortelen	carrots
zuurkool	sauerkraut

Sweets and desserts

appelgebak	apple tart or cake
gebak	pastry
ijs	ice cream
koekjes	biscuits
pannenkoeken	pancakes
pepernoten	ginger nuts
poffertjes	small pancakes, fritters
(slag)room	(whipped) cream
speculaas	spice and cinnamon-flavoured biscuit
stroopwafels	waffles
vla	custard

Fruits

aardbei	strawberry
amandel	almond
appel	apple
appelmoes	apple purée
citroen	lemon
druiven	grape
framboos	raspberry
kers	cherry
peer	pear
perzik	peach
pruim	plum/prune

Flemish specialities

hutsepot a winter-warmer consisting of various bits of beef and pork (often including pigs' trotters and ears) casseroled with turnips, celery, leeks and parsnips.

konijn met pruimen rabbit with prunes.

paling in 't groen eel braised in a green (usually spinach) sauce with herbs.

stoemp mashed potato mixed with vegetable and/or meat purée.

stoofvlees cubes of beef marinated in beer and cooked with herbs and onions.

stoverij stewed beef and offal (especially liver and kidneys), slowly tenderized in dark beer and served with a slice of bread covered in mustard.

waterzooi a delicious, filling soup-cum-stew, made with either chicken (*van kip*) or fish (*van riviervis*).

Drinks

anijsmelk	aniseed-flavoured warm milk
appelsap	apple juice
bessenjenever	blackcurrant gin
chocomel	chocolate milk
citroenjenever	lemon gin
droog	dry
frisdranken	soft drinks
jenever	a Dutch/Belgian gin
karnemelk	buttermilk
koffie	coffee
koffie verkeerd	coffee with warm milk
kopstoot	beer with a jenever chaser
melk	milk
met ijs	with ice
met slagroom	with whipped cream
pils	beer
prooot!	cheers!
sinaasappelsap	orange juice
thee	tea
tomatensap	tomato juice
vruchtensap	fruit juice
wijn	wine
(wit/rood/rosé)	(white/red/rosé)
vieux	Dutch brandy
zoet	sweet

Glossary

Dutch terms

Abdij Abbey

Begijnhof Convent occupied by beguines (*begijns*), i.e. members of a sisterhood living as nuns but without vows, retaining the right of return to the secular world. See box, p.75

Beiaard Carillon (i.e. a set of tuned church bells, either operated by an automatic mechanism or played by a keyboard)

BG (Begane grond) Ground floor ("basement" is K for kelder)

Belfort Belfry

Beurs Stock exchange

Botermarkt Butter market

Brug Bridge

Burgher Member of the upper or mercantile classes of a town, usually with certain civic powers

Geen toegang No entry

Gemeente Municipal, as in Gemeentehuis (town hall)

Gerechtshof Law Courts

Gesloten Closed

Gevel Gable: decoration on narrow-fronted canal houses

Gilde Guild

Gracht Canal

Groentenmarkt Vegetable market

(Grote) markt Central town square and the heart of most north Belgian communities, normally still the site of weekly markets

Hal Hall

Hof Courtyard

Huis House

Ingang Entrance

Jeugdherberg Youth hostel

Kaai Quay or wharf

Kapel Chapel

Kasteel Castle

Kerk Church; eg Grote Kerk – the principal church of the town

Koning King

Koningin Queen

Koninklijk Royal

Korenmarkt Corn market

Kunst Art

Lakenhal Cloth hall: the building in medieval weaving towns where cloth would be weighed, graded and sold

Let Op! Attention!

Luchthaven Airport

Molen Windmill

Noord North

Ommegang Procession

Onze Lieve Vrouwekerk or OLV Church of Our Lady

Oost East

Paleis Palace

Plaats/Plein A square or open space

Polder An area of land reclaimed from the sea

Poort Gate

Postbus Post box

Raadhuis Town hall

Rijk State

Schatkamer Treasury

Schepenzaal Alderman's Hall

Schone kunsten Fine arts

Schouwburg Theatre

Sierkunst Decorative arts

Spoor Track (as in railway) – trains arrive and depart on track (as distinct from platform) numbers

Stadhuis town hall

Stedelijk Civic, municipal

Steeg Alley

Steen Stone

Stichting Institute or foundation

Straat Street

Toegang Entrance

Toren Tower

Tuin Garden

Uitgang Exit

VA (Vanaf) "from"

Vleeshuis Meat market

Volkskunde Folklore

Weg Way

West West

Zuid South

Travel store

For more information go to www.roughguides.com

ROUGH
GUIDES

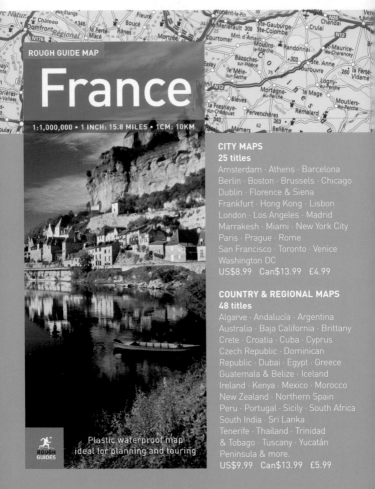

Get Connected!

"Brilliant! ... the unmatched leader in its field"
Sunday Times, London, reviewing The Rough Guide to the Internet

Rough Guide Computing Titles
Blogging • eBay • iPods, iTunes
& music online • The Internet
The iPhone • Macs & OS X • MySpace
Book of Playlists • PCs & Windows
PlayStation Portable • Website Directory

BROADEN YOUR HORIZONS

Visit us online
www.roughguides.com

Information on over 25,000 destinations around the world

- **Read** Rough Guides' trusted travel info

- **Access** exclusive articles from Rough Guides authors

- **Update** yourself on new books, maps, CDs and other products

- **Enter** our competitions and win travel prizes

- **Share** ideas, journals, photos & travel advice with other users

- **Earn** points every time you contribute to the Rough Guide
  community and get rewards

BROADEN YOUR HORIZONS

Listen Up!

"You may be used to the Rough Guide series being comprehensive, but nothing will prepare you for the exhaustive Rough Guide to World Music . . . one of our books of the year."

Sunday Times, London

Rough Guide Music Titles

The Beatles • Blues • Bob Dylan • Classical Music
Elvis • Frank Sinatra • Heavy Metal • Hip-Hop
iPods, iTunes & music online • Jazz • Book of Playlists
Led Zeppelin • Opera • Pink Floyd • Punk • Reggae
Rock • The Rolling Stones • Soul and R&B • World
Music Vol 1 & 2 • Velvet Underground

NOTES

small print & Index

A Rough Guide to Rough Guides

In 1981, Mark Ellingham, a recent graduate in English from Bristol University, was travelling in Greece on a tiny budget and couldn't find the right guidebook. With a group of friends he wrote his own guide, combining a contemporary, journalistic style with a practical approach to travellers' needs. That first Rough Guide was a student scheme that became a publishing phenomenon. Today, Rough Guides include recommendations from shoestring to luxury and cover hundreds of destinations around the globe, including almost every country in the Americas and Europe, more than half of Africa and most of Asia and Australasia. Millions of readers relish Rough Guides' wit and inquisitiveness as much as their enthusiastic, critical approach and value-for-money ethos. The guides' ever-growing team of authors and photographers is spread all over the world.

In the early 1990s, Rough Guides branched out of travel, with the publication of Rough Guides to World Music, Classical Music and the Internet. All three have become benchmark titles in their fields, spearheading the publication of a range of more than 350 titles under the Rough Guide name, including phrasebooks, waterproof maps, music guides from Opera to Heavy Metal, reference works as diverse as Conspiracy Theories and Shakespeare, and popular culture books from iPods to Poker. Rough Guides also produce a series of more than 120 World Music CDs in partnership with World Music Network.

Visit www.roughguides.com to see our latest publications.

Rough Guide travel images are available for commercial licensing at www.roughguidespictures.com

Publishing information

This second edition published May 2008 by
Rough Guides Ltd, 80 Strand, London WC2R 0RL.
345 Hudson St, 4th Floor, New York, NY 10014,
USA.

Distributed by the Penguin Group
Penguin Books Ltd, 80 Strand, London WC2R 0RL
Penguin Group (USA), 375 Hudson Street, NY
10014, USA
14 Local Shopping Centre, Panchsheel Park, New
Delhi 110017, India
Penguin Group (Australia), 250 Camberwell Road,
Camberwell, Victoria 3124, Australia
Penguin Group (Canada), 10 Alcorn Avenue,
Toronto, ON M4V 1E4, Canada
Penguin Group (NZ), 67 Apollo Drive, Mairangi Bay,
Auckland 1310, New Zealand
Typeset in Bembo and Helvetica to an original
design by Henry Iles.
Cover concept by Peter Dyer.

Printed and bound in China
© Phil Lee 2008

No part of this book may be reproduced in any
form without permission from the publisher except
for the quotation of brief passages in reviews.
192pp includes index
A catalogue record for this book is available from
the British Library
ISBN 978-1-85828-631-0

The publishers and authors have done their best
to ensure the accuracy and currency of all the
information in BRUGES & GHENT DIRECTIONS,
however, they can accept no responsibility for any
loss, injury, or inconvenience sustained by any
traveller as a result of information or advice
contained in the guide.

1   3   5   7   9   8   6   4   2

Help us update

We've gone to a lot of effort to ensure that the second edition of BRUGES & GHENT DIRECTIONS is accurate and up-to-date. However, things change – places get "discovered", opening hours are notoriously fickle, restaurants and rooms raise prices or lower standards. If you feel we've got it wrong or left something out, we'd like to know, and if you can remember the address, the price, the phone number, so much the better.

Please send your comments with the subject line "BRUGES & GHENT DIRECTIONS Update" to ✉mail@roughguides.com. We'll credit all contributions and send a copy of the next edition (or any other Rough Guide if you prefer) for the very best emails.

Have your questions answered and tell others about your trip at ✇community.roughguides.com.

Rough Guide credits

Text editor: Gavin Thomas
Layout: Jessica Subramanian
Photographers: Anthony Cassidy & Jean Christophe Godet
Cartography: Karobi Gogoi

Picture editor: Mark Thomas
Proofreader: Anne Durgot
Production: Rebecca Short
Cover design: Chloë Roberts

The author

Phil Lee has been writing for Rough Guides for well over fifteen years. His other books in the series include Canada, Norway, Amsterdam, Bruges, Mallorca, England and Toronto. He lives in Nottingham, where he was born and raised.

Acknowledgements

Phil Lee would like to thank his editor, Gavin Thomas, for his customary good humour and attention to detail during the preparation of this new edition of the *Directions Rough Guide to Bruges and Ghent*. Special thanks also to Katie Lloyd-Jones and Anita Rampall of Tourism Flanders & Brussels.

SMALL PRINT

Index

Maps are marked in colour. Note that in this index all Ghent entries are specified – those for Bruges are not.

INDEX